IGOR
STRAVINSKY
HIS LIFE AND TIMES

BY THE AUTHOR

Aaron Copland: His Life and Times
Igor Stravinsky: His Life and Times

IGOR STRAVINSKY

HIS LIFE AND TIMES

BY ARNOLD DOBRIN

Illustrated with Photographs

THOMAS Y. CROWELL COMPANY   NEW YORK

ACKNOWLEDGMENTS

The author wishes to make grateful acknowledgment to William Biegel, Jack Cash, Erik Johns, Ruth Steinkraus-Cohen, Aaron Copland, Sylvia Goldstein of Boosey & Hawkes, and Igor Stravinsky.

Grateful acknowledgment is made for permission to reprint quotations from *An Autobiography*, by Igor Stravinsky, Simon & Schuster, 1936; *Conversations with Igor Stravinsky*, by Igor Stravinsky and Robert Craft, Doubleday & Company, 1959, copyright © 1958, 1959 by Igor Stravinsky; *Dialogues and a Diary*, by Igor Stravinsky and Robert Craft, Doubleday & Company, 1963, copyright © 1961, 1962, 1963 by Igor Stravinsky, copyright © 1963 by Robert Craft.

MANUFACTURED IN THE UNITED STATES OF AMERICA

L.C. Card 77-101924

1   2   3   4   5   6   7   8   9   10

For Erik Johns

CONTENTS

IGOR STRAVINSKY

HIS LIFE AND TIMES

1

A RUSSIAN CHILDHOOD

At midday the heat of the Russian summer had silenced the birds, the people, even the giant horseflies that swarmed around the stables. Shades were drawn and the household tried to sleep or rest through the hottest hours. It was only later in the afternoon that the farm came to life as the peasants attended to their tasks around the country estate which belonged to Igor Stravinsky's aunt.

It was here in 1887, when he was only five, that one of the first vivid experiences of childhood etched itself so deeply into Igor's memory that it later seemed one of the most important events of these early years. Then he could easily recall the sharp, resinous tang of freshly cut wood in his nostrils, feel the soft, powdery dust of the farmyard beneath his feet, and watch, sweating in the oppressive heat, "an enormous peasant seated on the stump of a tree clad simply in a short red shirt." His bare legs were covered with reddish hair; on his feet he wore birch sandals; his head was covered with a mop of hair as thick and red as his beard. Though he was an old man, there were no white hairs.

Igor and the other children were frightened of him because he was mute and because he had a curious way of clicking his tongue very noisily. They tried to stay away from him but sometimes curiosity triumphed over fear and they would gather around him and watch his strange antics and listen to his wordless songs. Delighted by their attention, he attempted to hold it by singing a song that was composed of two syllables—the only two that he could pronounce.

"They were devoid of any meaning," Igor Stravinsky recalled, "but he made them alternate with incredible dexterity in a very rapid tempo." He could also make a certain sound that many children are familiar with by pressing the palm of his right hand under his left armpit and working his left arm with a rapid movement that pressed on the right hand.

"From beneath the red shirt he extracted a succession of sounds which were somewhat dubious but very rhythmic and which might be euphemistically described as resounding kisses." This noise amused and delighted Igor, who when he returned home tried to imitate the peasant's sounds and movements "so often and so successfully that I was forbidden to indulge in such indecent accompaniment."

Still another unforgettable memory of these early years was the songs of the women who lived in a neighboring village. For centuries folk songs have had an important place in Russian music. Ranging from sadness and nostalgia to gaiety and humor, they deeply appealed to the common people and, during the last years of the nineteenth century, also began to interest Russian musicians.

Like all peasant women of those years, these women spent a good part of each day—and all day during certain periods of the year—working in the fields. Regularly on the way home, in the early evening, they sang in unison, and Stravinsky once recalled that "to this day I clearly remember the tune, and the way they sang it, and how, when I used to sing it at home, imitating their manner, I was complimented on the trueness of my ear."

It was praise Igor needed, and he responded to it by developing the very abilities that had inspired it in the first place. His delight in the women's music had come spontaneously, and with that delight had come the impulse to imitate—to have the joy of making music himself.

This had drawn the approval and admiration of those two towering figures of childhood, his parents. And now the ground was firmly established which nurtures great musicians—an intuitive joy in music and enthusiastic approval of that joy. Aware of the importance of these early experiences, Stravinsky wrote, "Everyone was astonished and impressed. . . . I heard my father remark that I had a wonderful ear. I was pleased with my success, of course, and must have purred with pride." From these happy moments Stravinsky marked ". . . the dawn of my consciousness of myself in the role of musician."

In the years that lay ahead Igor's parents were to display a frustratingly ambivalent attitude toward the role of music in the life of their son. He was encouraged to attend operas and concerts and given piano lessons.

Igor's father was a professional singer who had left his law studies in the Niejinsky Lyceum as soon as he discovered that he had a good bass voice and a good musical ear. He had many friends in the world of music who came to the Stravinsky household and whom Igor saw there. He arranged for a pass so that his son could attend opera rehearsals and permitted him to study the numerous scores in his large music library.

And yet, after such an auspicious beginning, after years of experiences that inevitably drew Igor closer to the world of music, after allowing his interest to become passionate and demanding—after all this, Igor's parents refused to cooperate with him when the time came to make a decision about his future.

Feodor Stravinsky's determination to force his son into the profession of his choosing was not unusual. It was a rare Victorian father who would allow his son to pursue a career in the arts when any other alternative was possible, but the details that Stravinsky has recorded about his parents suggest that this was not simply the ordinary pattern of Victorian restrictions.

Igor's relations with his father had always been difficult. He was constantly frightened of him and of his outbursts of violent and uncontrollable temper that might explode at any moment.

Although he does not tell us the cause, later in life Igor Stravinsky could vividly recall a scene of terrible humiliation in a German resort town when, as a ten- or twelve-year-old child, he refused to immediately obey his father's order to return to the hotel. For the elder Stravinsky this was provocation enough to cause a major scandal in the street.

Circumstances were further complicated by the fact that Igor thought of his mother as a "distant parent." He understood his responsibilities toward his parents; he treated them with the respect and courtesy that were their due, but warmth, affection, love—these he received not from his mother but from Bertha, his nurse. It was because of Bertha—an East Prussian who knew almost no Russian—that German was the tongue spoken in the Stravinsky nursery.

The ties Igor formed with this warm and loving woman were deep and enduring. She left his employ only by death, in 1917, after having nursed his children and spent more than forty years with the Stravinsky family. "I mourned her," Igor wrote unashamedly, "more than I did, later, my mother."

Unfortunately the absence of love, and the emotional tension that strained Igor's relationship with his parents, also included his brothers. With the exception of his younger brother, Goury, Igor felt nothing for his brothers, and in later life he wrote—with an almost compulsive need to state the facts as baldly as possible —"When I remember my older brothers at all, it is to remind myself how exceedingly they used to annoy me."

Although a frail child, Igor was to outlive them all. Watched over constantly, scolded for the slightest infraction of the rules concerning his health, he was forbidden to participate in sports or games. "I suspect even now," he wrote in middle age, "my hatred of sports is my jealousy at having been deprived of them."

Stravinsky's brothers were stronger; they played games and appeared to have stamina. But Roman, the eldest, contracted diphtheria at eleven, which severely weakened his heart and killed him ten years later as he was concluding his law studies.

Youry became an architectural engineer and lived in Leningrad until his death in 1941. It was only with Goury, who had inherited his father's voice and musical ear, that Igor could feel any rapport. Goury had studied to be a singer and was about to embark on a promising career when he was conscripted into the Russian army during World War I. While in the service he contracted scarlet fever, from which he died in April 1917. Goury's death touched Igor, who wrote that ". . . news of it made me very lonely. We had been together constantly as children, and we felt that as long as we were together, all was well with the world. We found in each other the love and understanding denied us by our parents."

But even Goury had a small part in Stravinsky's memories of Russia—its vast forests, the long summers at the family's country estate, and St. Petersburg. He loved the sights, colors, and smells of this city—and especially its sounds, the street noises that varied from the rattles of carriages on the cobblestones to the calls of knife grinders, the cries of Russian and Tartar vendors, the cannonades of bells from nearby churches.

It was the custom of all families who could afford it to leave the city in the summer for their country estates. Here, in addition to the other pleasures of the outdoor life, were the wonderful summer fairs that dazzled the children and pleased even the sophisticated city visitors.

At Yarmolintsi, and later at the great fair of Nizhni Novgorod, Igor saw colorful exhibitions of peasant handicrafts, and sleek livestock, and the flashing, brilliant array of vividly patterned peasant costumes. He was awed by the crowds, noise, and dust, the fragrant odors of unfamiliar foods, the smell of horses and dung. "The Tartars . . . were always objects of mystery and fascination to me." Although they were exotic and foreign-looking, their business interests kept pace with the times: Igor could remember their asking "Nye pozhelayet'l marozhennoyeh?" (Would you like some ice cream?) Above all he delighted in the dancing contests, where for the first time he saw the *presiatka* (heel dance) and the *kazachock* (clicking dance), both of which were to delight audiences in the last scenes of his ballet *Pétrouchka.*

Often summers were spent with his Aunt Sophie and Uncle Alexander Ielatchitch, who had married five years before his own parents. The five children of this marriage "were therefore just enough older than the four of us to insure that we suffered an ample amount of taunting and misery."

But if the cousins may have inflicted the usual number of juvenile tortures upon each other, they were not enough to cloud what were to be some of Igor Stravinsky's happiest childhood memories.

When they returned to St. Petersburg for the fall and winter season the Stravinsky family occupied a large and luxurious flat in a building at 66 Krukov Canal. Although Igor was born (on June 17, 1882) at Oranienbaum on the Gulf of Finland, this apartment was to remain his home during his boyhood and youth. From his bedroom window Igor could see barges carrying scenery for the Maryinsky Theater. Through the long Russian winters the canal froze solid and became a busy thoroughfare for sleds.

The flat was furnished with heavy, dark pieces of furniture in the usual Victorian manner. There were velvet draperies, a profusion of detail, mauve upholstery, and sentimental paintings. But unlike most Victorian homes, the apartment possessed an unusual library and two grand pianos.

Igor's parents did not concern themselves with his musical education until he was nine. Then they hired Mlle. Kashperova, who had been a student of Anton Rubinstein and was a well-known teacher in St. Petersburg. Igor very quickly learned to read music and soon began to improvise. Before long he was devoting the largest part of his free time to the pleasures of improvisation.

To his parents and Mlle. Kashperova this was merely a waste of time. He was often reprimanded for his lack of discipline, and this caused a good deal of friction. But Igor could not easily agree to exchange the delight of his own improvisations for the wearisome practice his teacher demanded.

It was to be many years before Stravinsky could understand and admit the need of such discipline for a child of nine or ten. Although he finally acknowledged it, in later life he still maintained that these hours of constant improvisation had sowed the seed of many musical ideas that later came to fruition.

By the time he was sixteen he could play the Mendelssohn G Minor Concerto with Mlle. Kashperova, sonatas by Mozart and Haydn, Beethoven, Schubert, and Schumann. Chopin was forbidden, and Mlle. Kashperova tried to discourage his interest in Wagner.

One of his teacher's idiosyncrasies was to forbid him the use of the pedals under any circumstances; because of this, as well as other demands, she is one of the targets of the deep resentment that Stravinsky revealed in his autobiography. He thought that her narrowness and rigidity contributed to the bitterness of his mid-twenties, a bitterness that included his schools, his studies, his family, and his teachers. Summing up, he wrote that his childhood was "a period of waiting for the moment when I could send everyone and everything connected with it to hell."

A large part of the unhappiness of these early years could be attributed to the unpleasant experiences Igor suffered at school. After first attending a government school he changed to a St. Petersburg gymnasium, where he remained until he was fifteen. Then he went to a private school called the Gourévitch Gymnasium about eight miles from the Stravinsky home. As he was usually too late to take the tram to school, Igor paid forty or fifty kopecks to hire a fiacre, which was, he wrote, the best thing about going to school.

Especially in the winter, on the way home, it was a great pleasure to drive through the Nevsky Prospekt in a sleigh, protected by a net from the dirty snow kicked up by the horses, and then, at home, to warm himself in front of the big white porcelain stove.

At the Gourévitch school Igor studied history, Latin, Greek, Russian and French literature, and mathematics;

he detested these studies and was not to change his attitude as he grew older or entered different schools.

There was never enough time to waste it on subjects that were dull compared to the infinite pleasures of music—of talking about it, listening to it, composing it oneself. The more Igor went to concerts and operas the more he wanted to go.

The first opera he attended was Mikhail Glinka's *A Life for the Tsar,* but already he was familiar with much of the music. That this experience left an indelible impression was partly due to Glinka's music but also because this was Igor's first hearing of a full orchestra.

Later Stravinsky wrote of Glinka:

His orchestration . . . remains a perfect monument to musical art—so intelligent is his balance of tone, so distinguished and delicate his instrumentations and by the latter I mean his choice of instruments and his way of combining them. I was indeed fortunate in happening upon a chef d'oeuvre for my first contact with great music. That is why my attitude towards Glinka has always been one of unbounded gratitude.

Later Igor went to hear Glinka's second opera, *Ruslan and Ludmilla,* at a gala performance given to celebrate its fiftieth anniversary. Although the music was exciting, and his father had an important part, the high point of the evening came when Igor caught a glimpse of Peter Tchaikovsky in the foyer: ". . . the idol of the Russian public, whom I had never seen before and was never to see again."

At the age of seven or eight he had seen Tchaikovsky's ballet *The Sleeping Beauty* and had been enchanted. He had already known a good deal about this work before seeing it in the theater; in fact, in addition to being familiar with much of the music and plot he could also identify some of the dance positions of the classical ballet.

But the pleasures of the concert hall or opera could not relieve the unhappiness that clouded Igor Stravinsky's early years. His father's seemingly irrational rages continued, and the days when he was to perform were worst of all. At these times he took his meals apart from the rest of the family and the slightest upset would provoke an irritable outburst. Igor's mother remained a remote figure who appeared to have little time for her son.

All his love was directed to Bertha and to his homeland—the vast and marvelous beauty of Russia. When asked as an old man what he loved most in Russia during these years Stravinsky replied, "The violent Russian spring that seemed to begin in an hour and was like the whole earth cracking. That was the most wonderful event of every year of my childhood."

2

YOUTH IN ST. PETERSBURG

Loneliness dominated Igor Stravinsky's early years. His hatred of school had made him a poor pupil, which only intensified his parents' reproaches and gave rise to an increasing number of disagreeable scenes. There was nowhere to take refuge—certainly not at school, only rarely at home. Like many other artists who have found their early years painful, he found that his sense of alienation only perpetuated his dislike of school and the disciplines to which he could not and would not submit. Worst of all, there was no one to confide in, to talk to, no one to whom he could pour out his longings and despair—not even Goury, of whom Igor was very fond. The affection the brothers felt for each other remained on the surface; each appeared to fear any real intimacy or friendship.

It was only as Igor grew into adolescence that he found a place where his budding ambitions and dreams were understood and encouraged—the house of Uncle Ielatchitch. The Ielatchitch family prided themselves on their liberal outlook, were extremely interested in social reform and opposed to the tyrannical government of the czar. Most important, all members of this household were fervent music lovers who did not lavish all their praise on the masterpieces of the past but were also interested in contemporary developments.

With the Ielatchitch family Igor attended as many symphony concerts and recitals as possible and heard most of the prominent performers and conductors of his time. These events were sponsored by the Imperial Musical Society or the Russian Symphony Concerts; for the most part their programs were staid and unimaginative. But not having yet developed any critical faculty, Igor was delighted and impressed with everything he heard.

Very quickly he became an ardent admirer of Nikolai Rimsky-Korsakov because of his beautiful orchestration and distinctive melodic invention. Alexander Glazunov, then at the height of his fame, appealed to Igor because of his feeling for symphonic form.

Soon a young friend, Ivan Pokrovsky, older than himself and highly cultured, introduced Igor to contemporary composers from abroad—especially the music of Gounod, Bizet, Delibes, and Chabrier. The work of these men was a revelation of new musical concepts and a world that was totally foreign to the Russian musical tradition.

The aspiring composer was fascinated with their harmonic methods, their conceptions of melody, and their new, free feeling for form. Hearing their music also aroused Igor's interest in western European culture; it stimulated his curiosity and it made him only more impatient with the drab daily round of school and home life in St. Petersburg.

For some time now there had been talk of what profession Igor should begin to prepare for. Curiously, even though his father was a professional musician, Igor's parents, like most people of their class, considered a profession in the arts most improper and insecure. Perhaps Feodor Stravinsky's experiences in the musical world embittered him. Perhaps he wanted to save his son from similar experiences.

Whatever the reasons, and paradoxical as they may sound, Igor's parents were firmly set against his hopes of becoming a composer. Obviously it was a precarious vocation; even worse was the risk of falling into a dissolute Bohemian existence. The Stravinskys were convinced that their son's education should enable him to obtain a post—administrative or otherwise—that would assure him of a good livelihood and enable him to maintain the standard of living he had known in childhood. They acknowledged his interest in music but did not encourage it. No discussion about the matter would be tolerated; as soon as he was ready Igor entered the University of St. Petersburg to begin the study of law.

Stravinsky did as his parents wished but with a smoldering rebelliousness that refused to be extinguished. Lectures were optional, so Igor "opted not to attend." In his entire four years at the university he estimated that he probably didn't hear more than fifty lectures. He read both criminal law and legal philosophy, and though he was interested in the theoretical and abstract questions of both, his absorption in music had accelerated to such a degree that he had little thought left over for his law studies.

Already Stravinsky's concern for literature had become well developed through wide and eclectic reading. Although Dostoevski was his "hero," he also admired the Danish playwright August Strindberg, the plays of the Norwegian Henrik Ibsen, the works of Charles Dickens and Mark Twain.

Fortunately, Igor's parents did not prevent more advanced musical studies even while he continued his study of law. He began to study harmony but unexpectedly found little satisfaction in it. Although he suspected this might be due to his teacher's incompetence he probably realized even then that the real reason was his intense aversion to tedious study.

Igor's probing, quick, adventuresome mind did not like the disciplines of such study and in his autobiography he unequivocably stated:

Let me make myself clear. I always did, and still do, prefer to achieve my aims and to solve any problems which confront me in the course of my work solely by my own efforts, without having recourse to established processes which do, it is true, facilitate the task, but which must first be learned and then remembered. To learn and remember such things, however useful they might be, always seemed to me dull and boring.

Further on he suggests that some elements of pleasure must be integral to all work and study, that without it, nothing of an enduring or meaningful nature can be achieved.

But another musical discipline often considered dry—
that of counterpoint—had an immediate fascination for
the young composer. From the age of eighteen he began to study it alone from an ordinary manual. It was
so absorbing that he never tired of it; far more than
harmony, it appeared to open vast horizons of possibility and challenge.

Later he realized how profoundly this earlier study
had developed his musical discrimination, taste, and
understanding. As so often happens, the discipline that
he imposed willingly on himself not only gave him intense enjoyment but greatly developed his creativity
and skill. These exercises in counterpoint stimulated his
imagination and increased his desire to compose. He
believed they had laid the foundation of his future
techniques and prepared him thoroughly for the studies
of orchestration, form, and instrumentation that he later
undertook with Rimsky-Korsakov.

The most exciting time of the week came when he
attended a new series of concerts called "Evenings of
Contemporary Music." Here, for the first time, he heard
the flowing, sensuous music of the French Impressionists, Debussy and Ravel. Although it seemed contradic-
tory to the name of the series, pre-Bach music was also
played; the work of Monteverdi, Couperin, and other
eighteenth-century masters opened up a new and unexpected world.

Igor Stravinsky was ready for a real guide into the
musical world, a teacher who could further his com-
prehension of the basic elements of his art while

nurturing his highly individual talents. In 1902 he was to meet this teacher, a man who was not only one of the great composers of his time, but one with whom he could also form a happy personal relationship. During the summer of this year, Igor's father, already ill with the disease that would kill him, had gone to Bad Wildungen in Germany to take a cure. His family, including the reluctant Igor, naturally accompanied him. Unexpectedly, shortly after their arrival, Igor found that another visitor was staying near Bad Wildungen, one who was to make it a memorable summer.

Nikolai Rimsky-Korsakov had come with his family to spend the summer at nearby Heidelberg, where one of his sons was a student at the university—a young man whom Igor had known when they were fellow students in St. Petersburg. At once Igor dashed over to see his old friend, and, not incidentally, meet his famous father.

Rimsky-Korsakov was tall, nervous, and asthmatic. Because of poor eyesight he wore blue-tinted glasses and sometimes kept an extra pair on his forehead—a habit that was later copied by Stravinsky. Although a member of the upper class, he was a radical unalterably opposed to the oppressive czarist regime. Igor was delighted to learn that Rimsky—as he sometimes referred to him—was witty and had a lively sense of humor.

With the candor and impetuousness of youth he soon asked the older man's advice about entering the world of music as a composer. Before answering, Rimsky-Korsakov asked Igor to play some of his first compositions. Igor began eagerly to play, but ". . . the way in which he received them was far from what I had hoped. Seeing how upset I was, and evidently anxious not to discourage me, he asked if I could play anything else. I did so, of course, and it was then that he gave his opinion."

Rimsky-Korsakov said that it was of the first importance that Igor continue his study of harmony—a discipline that was essential if he was to acquire mastery of the art he had chosen. Still, he advised him *not* to enter the Conservatory. As a professor there he must have realized at once that its stolid, traditional atmosphere would not be suited to the temperament of the young composer.

With gentleness and tact, Rimsky-Korsakov suggested that Igor continue with his law courses at the university and concluded the interview by saying that he should always feel free to come whenever he wanted advice. When Igor had acquired the necessary musical foundation, Rimsky would be glad to give him more direction and help.

Igor was downcast at such a lukewarm reception—especially one that pointed the way to more long, dreary hours of studying harmony. He resolved at once to plunge into this study again but found, just as quickly, that it made him as bored and restless as before.

And yet—painful as this work was—Igor gradually began to master it; the day was not far off when Rimsky-Korsakov would agree to give him further instruction.

3

STUDY WITH
RIMSKY-KORSAKOV

When Igor Stravinsky went to visit Rimsky-Korsakov
at his summer home in the summer of 1903 the orchards
were heavy with ripening peaches and cherries, the
peasants were ruddy from their work in the fields, and
the countryside had an atmosphere of fruitful peace-
fulness. Yet Igor felt anything but peaceful as he
checked and rechecked to see that the score of his first
full-sized sonata for the piano was securely tucked in
the bottom of his bag.

After the usual greetings and an exchange of news,
Igor sat down at the piano. He was too engrossed in
playing to note Rimsky-Korsakov's reaction, but when
he finished and the composer began to speak, he knew
that the response would not be enthusiastic. After a few
brief comments Rimsky instructed Igor in the principles
of the allegro of a sonata and then made him compose
the first part of a sonatina under his supervision. Later
Stravinsky recalled, "He explained these principles with
a lucidity so remarkable as to show me at once what a
great teacher he was."

On the following days Rimsky-Korsakov showed him

a good many more aspects of the art of musical composition. He instructed him in the tonal range and registers of the different instruments that are used by modern symphonic orchestras; he revealed the basic elements of orchestration. "Always his approach was to teach form and orchestration side by side because he believed that the more highly developed musical forms find their fullest expression in the complexity of the orchestra."

Sometimes Rimsky would give Igor the piano score of a new work he had just finished and would ask him to arrange it for an orchestra. When he finished, the composer would show him his own orchestration of these same passages.

After studying and comparing them Igor would be asked to explain the reasons why he believed Rimsky had chosen to work in the manner revealed by the finished score. Igor's answers were perceptive and he learned quickly; before his visit came to a close Rimsky-Korsakov agreed to begin regular lessons in the fall after their return to St. Petersburg.

One of the conditions Rimsky-Korsakov insisted upon was that Igor continue his studies of counterpoint with his former teacher, who had himself once been a student of Rimsky-Korsakov's. Igor tried to comply with this condition but after a short time he decided that he would be able to learn more studying by himself.

Much of the work with Rimsky continued to be assignments to orchestrate classical music—often sections of Beethoven's sonatas and Schubert's quartets. Rimsky-

Korsakov had published an important book on instrumentation and was particularly strong in this area; perhaps the most important part of his instruction was his emphasis on giving Igor a deep understanding of the color and full range of each instrument.

Rimsky-Korsakov was one of the famous Five who began, in the 1860's, to exert an important influence on the course of Russian music. (The others were Mily Balakireff, César Cui, Alexander Borodin, and Modest Moussorgsky.) Tchaikovsky, a contemporary, was not included in the group because his ties to German music were strong and The Five wanted, above all, to express the Russian spirit. During the last years of the nineteenth century, when a growing nationalism swept across Europe, The Five turned to the life of the ordinary Russian man for inspiration. They explored Russian folktales, legends, and history; through these interests and their determination and talent emerged the first truly Russian school of music.

Once a week Stravinsky took his work to his teacher for criticism and correction; afterward they carefully analyzed the form and structure of different classical works. Although Stravinsky was grateful to Rimsky-Korsakov for the many things he taught him, he remained convinced that the most important knowledge about composition had to be discovered by himself.

Many years later he wrote of Rimsky-Korsakov: "His knowledge was precise, and he was able to impart whatever he knew with great clarity. His teaching was all 'technical'. But whereas he knew valuable details

about harmony and practical orchestral writing, what
he knew about composition itself was not all it should
have been."

Still, he was interested in his teacher's thoughts about
all aspects of musicianship. One day he asked Rimsky-
Korsakov if he was right in composing at the piano.
"Some compose at the piano," his teacher replied, "and
some without a piano. As for you, you will compose at
the piano." (Stravinsky always maintained it was the
best and proper way to compose.)

After a year of work with Rimsky-Korsakov, Stravinsky was eager to begin a more ambitious work than the
small pieces that had occupied him up to now. Confi-
dent that he could bring it off, he began his first symphony, and showed his teacher each part as soon as it
was finished.

Highly derivative—as was to be expected—the symphony showed the influence of Tchaikovsky, Wagner, Rimsky-Korsakov, and especially Glazunov, who
"reigned supreme in the science of the symphony at
that time." During these years, the height of Glazunov's
popularity, Stravinsky recalled that "each new production of his was received as a musical event of the first
order, so great were the perfection of his form, the purity of his counterpoint. . . . I shared this admiration
wholeheartedly, fascinated by the astonishing mastery
of this scholar."

In the meantime, Stravinsky's relationship with Rimsky-Korsakov was far from that of the usual pupil-
master variety. He quickly made friends with the

teacher's entire family and often dined with them after his lesson.

The cultured environment in which they moved allowed Igor to form many new ties with young people who were interested not only in music but in many of the other arts as well. There were young scientists, scholars, painters—people who were intensely concerned with contemporary developments both at home and abroad.

Igor Stravinsky wrote that ". . . we took a passionate interest in everything that went on in the intellectual and artistic life of the capital." Rimsky himself, however, took a staunchly conservative attitude toward new developments in the world of art and cautioned Stravinsky, while at a concert at which music by Debussy was performed, "Better not listen to him; one runs the risk of getting accustomed to him and one would end by liking him."

Stravinsky, who would not be influenced by such unyielding conservatism, believed that Debussy would soon capture the world with his enchanting music, which seemed to have "extraordinary freedom and freshness of technique." After Debussy it was the music of Chabrier that seemed to him most vigorous and contemporary.

Igor was impatient to join the ranks of composers whose works were being performed, discussed, and reviewed. "I felt an imperative need to get a foothold in my profession," he wrote, realizing, at the same time, that he must still continue to study the established musicians of the past.

The technical knowledge that I acquired, thanks to them, gave me a foundation of incalculable value in its solidity, on which I was able later to establish and develop my craftsmanship. No matter what the subject may be, there is only one course for the beginner; he must at first accept a discipline imposed from without, but only as a means of obtaining freedom for and strengthening himself in his own method of expression.

With such insistence upon finding his own way, Igor Stravinsky must have been glad when the weekly lesson ended and the social evening with the Rimsky-Korsakovs and their friends began.

It was from the great composer that Igor first heard English spoken. Rimsky-Korsakov often liked to use this language in conversational asides. One day, when Stravinsky was present, a young composer excitedly told Rimsky that he had lost the score of his new work in the carriage—the very score that he had come to show his teacher. Rimsky groaned his disappointment in Russian but whispered to Stravinsky in English, "The heavens are merciful."

The Rimsky-Korsakovs lived well and ate well. There were always copious servings of vodka and *zalousky* (snacks of mushrooms, ham, and other delicacies), after which everyone went in to eat a large and excellent dinner. The conversation moved swiftly from one subject to another, except for one that was always forbidden.

Igor soon learned that Rimsky-Korsakov's mind was "closed to any religious or metaphysical idea. If the conversation happened to touch on some point of religion or philosophy he would simply refuse to allow that point to be considered in the light of revealed religion."

One night, when someone introduced the subject of life after death into the conversation, Rimsky's response was to draw a zero on the tablecloth. He looked straight ahead and said emphatically, "There is nothing after death; death is the end."

When Igor ventured to suggest that this was only his point of view Rimsky-Korsakov made it clear, both on this and future occasions, that he would have been wiser not to have said it.

The circumstances of Igor Stravinsky's life were changing rapidly; no longer was he a bored and miserable child but a young man quickly making strides in his chosen art.

After the death of his father in 1902 a new, more relaxed life began for Igor. He immediately enjoyed greater freedom and it seemed that at last he might be able to make an adjustment to life at home. Unfortunately his problems with his mother seemed to grow worse, until he finally left home to seek refuge with a newly married cousin.

With a deep-seated bitterness that remained with him fifty years afterward he recalled: "After a few days my mother managed to fall ill enough to force me to come back. She did behave slightly less egotistically after that, however, and her delight in torturing me seemed slightly less intense."

Certainly Mme. Stravinsky's plans for her son's future could not be enforced as they had been before her husband's death. Igor was gaining more independence with every day; he would have to remain at the university until he finished his law courses, but already it was becoming clear to everyone that he was destined for an entirely different kind of life than that of the law courts and offices.

4

THE MOMENTUM
QUICKENS

The year 1905 was a momentous one for both Igor Stravinsky and for Russia. During this year he finished his courses at the university in St. Petersburg, and in the autumn his engagement to Catherine Nossenko, his first cousin, was announced at the Nossenko country house.

Catherine, a year older than Igor, had been an almost constant friend from the age of ten. "From our first hour together," Igor said, "we both seemed to realize that we would one day marry—or so we told each other later." When they became adolescents, their feeling for each other deepened and now, in their early twenties, they eagerly looked forward to marriage.

Catherine was a pretty girl with light blue eyes and brown hair lighted by golden tints. She had lived in Paris and studied voice; Igor could see that music was one of the most important things in her life. She was a gifted music calligrapher and later became Stravinsky's best copyist.

Igor had reddish brown hair and wore a rather serious expression in spite of his love for amusements and the other pleasures of life. He was a small man—only five feet four inches—but like many other men of small stature, he was well developed and strong. Often moving about quickly, he seemed to express in his very gait and gestures the inner tension and vibrant energy that was soon to be heard in his music.

No sooner had the young couple announced their determination to marry than a number of serious problems arose because of an imperial Russian statute that forbade the marriage of first cousins.

Igor was greatly occupied with these difficulties, and concerned by his family's disapproval, but that autumn, as he began the journey back to St. Petersburg, he could not escape the realization that his future life—married or not—was to be profoundly influenced by the course of events which were leading Russia to great changes.

In the summer of 1905 the crew of the Russian battleship *Potemkin* had mutinied, and the sympathetic strikes that followed created a dangerous situation throughout the country. The mood of rebellion was strong and filtering through to all levels of society. For a time the postal service was disrupted and in the major cities soldiers stood guard before government buildings. Because of the strike in the railway system Igor found it almost impossible to get a train from the country back into the city; once he found a seat he realized that the growing apprehension and alarm of the people could easily get out of hand.

There were good reasons for the desperation felt not only by the Russian peasantry but by the middle class as well. As late as 1897 census reports indicated that almost four fifths of the Russian people were unable to read or write. It is estimated that by the end of the nineteenth century not more than 150,000 boys and 100,000 girls were enrolled in the separate secondary schools maintained by the government. For many centuries a vast population of uneducated masses and a very small educated elite were features of the traditional scheme of things in Russia, and the aristocracy deeply feared the consequences of education for the peasants.

Early in 1905, without a declaration of war, the Japanese attacked Port Arthur in southern Manchuria and destroyed the Russian squadron based there. The Russo-Japanese war that was the consequence of this attack lasted for more than a year and seriously lowered the morale of the Russian people, who were shaken by their country's defeat.

But this was only one of the many grievances festering in Russian society. Its awakening can be traced to the eighteenth century, which produced many critics of society, many enlightened reformers who worked to change the old, inequitable order of things.

Some of these men were poets and visionaries; others were aggressive, determined revolutionaries who believed that any and all means, including violence, must be used to achieve social reform. Even before the time of the German socialist Karl Marx all the ideas and institutions associated with the czarist aristocracy were being criticized and attacked. Then, as the nineteenth century drew to a close, this attack began to swell into a violent storm that swept across the land.

Igor Stravinsky was not interested in politics at this or any future time in his life. Still, he could not be immune to the climate of change and disorder. Only two things were certain for him during this period: one, that he would let nothing interfere with his musical career, and two, that he would marry Catherine Nossenko in spite of prohibitions from the state, the Church, and members of both their families.

Because of the imperial statute forbidding marriage between first cousins it was almost impossible to find a priest who would consent to marry them. Finally one was found who agreed to officiate at the ceremony without demanding to see the documents that revealed the close relationship between Catherine and Igor. Their marriage finally took place on January 11, 1906, in the small village of Novaya Derevnya near St. Petersburg, with not one member of their families present. The only attendants were Andrei and Vladimir Rimsky-Korsakov, sons of the composer.

Meanwhile, Igor's lessons with Rimsky-Korsakov had continued as usual. Relations with the composer's family had also grown more cordial and the social gatherings increased in number. It was at one of their parties that Igor met Scriabin, a composer who was then enjoying a great vogue in Russia but whose music Igor did not like. The brilliant young musician Sergei Prokofiev, only seventeen or eighteen years old, was a frequent guest as well.

Although they liked each other and continued to see each other through the coming years, Stravinsky felt that Prokofiev was the sort of fellow "one could see a thousand times without establishing any profound connection with him . . . and we rarely discussed music when we were together. I used to think that Prokofiev's depths were engaged only when he played chess. He was a master player. . . . Prokofiev had that rare thing, the instant imprint of personality. . . ."

Igor Stravinsky was working with great determination, and works were beginning to come from his pen in astonishing numbers. A small symphony (Opus 1), highly academic and owing much to Brahms, was dedicated to Rimsky-Korsakov. One of his first compositions to be performed was the impressionist *Le Faune et la Bergère,* a suite of songs for mezzo-soprano and orchestra.

Several works were also in progress, including the *Scherzo Fantastique* and the first act of his opera *The Nightingale,* the libretto of which—based on a story by Hans Christian Andersen—Igor wrote in collaboration with his good friend S. Mitusov.

Rimsky-Korsakov encouraged him after seeing preliminary sketches for this work but did not live to see the finished composition. He was already a victim of the heart disease that was soon to kill him.

The presentation of the *Scherzo Fantastique* and *Fireworks* during the winter season of 1909 marked a turning point in Stravinsky's life. In the audience one night was a large, self-possessed man with a face that reminded one of a bulldog. He spoke fluent French, had a cultured voice, and obviously possessed considerable wealth. It was Sergei Diaghilev—soon to become one of the greatest impresarios the world would know.

As artistic director of the Russian Ballet (Ballet Russe) he was entirely responsible for the conception and production of its entire repertoire.

Diaghilev liked Stravinsky's compositions, he liked the fresh new rhythms and especially the glittering cascades of sound he heard in *Fireworks.* This music conjured a vivid atmosphere of pinwheels gaily whirling, of rockets streaming across the sky, and of sparks falling in bright showers. It was a highly inventive and compelling new work, in which one could hear the arresting rhythms that would change musical history.

Soon after the performance Diaghilev asked Stravinsky to orchestrate two pieces by Chopin for the Russian Ballet, thus beginning an important relationship that was to last for twenty years.

Although he was pleased with Stravinsky's work, Diaghilev offered him no further commissions, and Igor returned to his house in the country, where he resumed work on *The Nightingale.* He was deeply engrossed in it and planned, after the customary autumnal return to St. Petersburg, to continue work on what was his most ambitious project thus far. But no sooner had he returned to the city when a telegram arrived that was to have enormous importance to his future career. It was a request from Sergei Diaghilev to write the score of *The Firebird* for the next season of the Russian Ballet.

5

EARLY TRIUMPHS WITH
THE RUSSIAN BALLET

"Etonne moi" (Surprise me), Sergei Diaghilev told
Jean Cocteau when discussing future works the French
writer-director-poet was preparing for the Russian Ballet. Simple words, yet they succinctly conveyed the
great entrepreneur's love of the new, the fresh, and
the original.

Sergei Pavlovitch Diaghilev had first become an important figure in the art world when he established an
art magazine in Moscow called *Mir Iskusstva* (World
of Art). In 1906 he arranged a large exhibition of Russian art in the Grand Palais in Paris. For the most part
it consisted of traditional works but it also included the
work of contemporary artists and designers such as
Léon Bakst and Alexandre Benois—brilliantly colored,
dramatic works with which the theater-going public
was soon to become acquainted; these men were among
the first Diaghilev was to commission to design the
sets and costumes for the Russian Ballet. But even before their work enhanced and magnified the dynamic
impression created by the Russian Ballet it aroused
much comment and controversy in Parisian art circles.

This was the kind of talk and notoriety Diaghilev loved and needed; from these first years in Paris until his last, Diaghilev was a presence—he and his productions were news. Wherever Diaghilev went he created an air of excitement, of the unique, of something special about to happen.

Even physically he was uncommon. Sergei Diaghilev was a big man, slightly more than six feet tall, broad and big-limbed but not corpulent. The most striking thing about him was the disproportionate size of his head. Composer Vladimir Dukelsky wrote, "His head was enormous, and the face—a world in itself." Cocteau said that Diaghilev seemed to wear "the smallest hat in creation—yet it only appeared small because of his huge head."

During early youth a streak of pale silver hair had sprung from the middle of his hairline to accent this memorable head. Because of it his dancers nicknamed him "Chinchilla."

Diaghilev's eyes had a piercing, mocking intensity about them, accented by unusually heavy eyelids. He wore a small, close-clipped mustache and carried a large variety of monocles, which, in the manner of the time, he slowly screwed into one eye when he wanted to exaggerate a lofty announcement or focus his attention on something. He spoke French and English, as well as Russian, with a somewhat affected, aristocratic accent.

Stravinsky wrote that Diaghilev was "in no sense an intellectual . . . he was much too sensual for that. . . ." And yet, everyone seems to agree that he was one of the most cultured men of his time, and in his special field, the history of Russian painting, an acknowledged and respected scholar. He had been a bibliophile all his life and owned a library of Russian literature that was considered one of the finest in the world. Unlike many other connoisseurs who steep themselves in the history of art, Diaghilev also had an intense interest in contemporary developments. He always fought against dogmatic beliefs and against the cultural bureaucracy, which generally supports old traditions. One of his friends wrote that "tomorrow" was the watchword of all his activities.

Diaghilev was extremely superstitious, carried amulets and talismans, and pronounced magic formulas to destroy evil influences or to create good ones. He could not tolerate the number thirteen and loathed black cats. He was terrified of the *mal occhio* (the evil eye) and would make the ancient sign with the index and little fingers of his right hand whenever he thought he was in the presence of someone who possessed it.

Once when Stravinsky and Diaghilev were having a conversation in a theater Stravinsky noticed that Diaghilev was using his left hand to gesticulate but holding his right hand close to his side in the sign that is supposed to destroy the power of the *mal occhio*. "Seriosha, what are you doing?" asked Stravinsky.

Diaghilev pointed to the three men behind him and whispered that one of them had the *mal occhio;* he steadfastly refused to move the fingers of his hand until they had left.

Buoyed by the reception that the Russian painters

had received during the exhibition of 1906, Diaghilev decided to organize a performance of the Russian Ballet for Western audiences. It was a particularly propitious moment because France at this time was receptive to foreign cultural influences; the prevailing climate was one of peace and good fellowship.

Russia, which was still largely unknown in the West, was viewed as a mysterious semi-Asiatic country. The English writer Arthur Symons conveyed the attitude of many when he wrote in 1904:

Other races, too long civilized, have accustomed themselves to the soul, to mystery, to whatever is most surprising in life and death. Russia, with centuries of savagery behind it, still feels the earth about its roots, or the thirst in it of the primitive animal. It has lost none of its instincts and it has just discovered its strange soul . . . it is ceaselessly disturbed by that strange inner companion. . . .

Partly because of such attitudes toward Russia, theater audiences awaited the Russian Ballet with a receptive, hospitable attitude. But no preconceived ideas could possibly have prepared them for the enormous revelation of this unfamiliar culture.

To describe the first performances of the Ballet in 1909 as a success, even a glittering or great success, would be a gross understatement. With its brilliant scenery and magnificent dancing and music the Russian Ballet revealed a world that had been thought part of the distant and unrecapturable past.

Even before the dancing began—when the audience had only time to observe the first stage-drops of vivid

Oriental colors—an electric current seemed to surge through the theater. The intense colors seemed to echo the first chords of the ballet music. When the dancers appeared they revealed a skill and artistry that Paris had never seen before.

Years later members of these earliest audiences wrote in their memoirs that their first experience of the Russian Ballet was one of the extraordinary events of their lives. In these memoirs, diaries, and journals one superlative succeeds another in the hope of communicating what this theatrical event meant to audiences.

The advent of the Ballet Russe [wrote one enthusiast] was an event in the truest sense of the word, a shock of surprise, a whirlwind, a new impact. . . . I may say without exaggeration that my life is split into two epochs; before and after the Russian Ballet! All our ideas underwent a change. It was as though the scales had fallen from our eyes.

Twenty years later the Countess de Noailles wrote:

When I entered the box to which I had been invited, I arrived slightly late, not altogether believing in the revelation certain initiates had promised me; but I realized at once that something miraculous was happening, that I was witnessing something absolutely unique. Everything that could strike the imagination, intoxicate, enchant, and win one over seemed to have been assembled on that stage. . . .

Diaghilev was of course delighted by these early successes and immediately began to plan new productions for the 1910 season.

His choreographer, Michel Fokine, had been planning a new ballet based on the ancient Russian legend of the *Zhar-Ptitsa*—a magical bird with wings of flame. The Russian composer Anatole Liadov had agreed to compose the score but continued to be overwhelmed by the procrastination that seriously troubled him throughout his life.

When Diaghilev discovered six months later that Liadov had not written even a note of the new score he was furious—particularly since he was obsessed by the idea that the next season of the ballet must be even more impressive than the first had been.

He was determined to present the world with the most magnificent theatrical presentations it had ever witnessed; of course these efforts were wildly expensive and of course he always exceeded his budget. And yet—unlike many entrepreneurs, who have eyes only for the greatest names, who will associate themselves only with established reputations—Diaghilev was constantly on the lookout for the unknown, the obscure talent that was waiting to be discovered, encouraged, allowed to grow and, eventually, to dazzle. It was at this point that Diaghilev remembered the young man whose composition of such verve and fire had been played at the Siloti concert in St. Petersburg.

When the momentous telegram arrived Stravinsky was tremendously excited but, like all young artists just beginning their careers, he was filled with anxiety. Could he bring it off to his own and Diaghilev's satisfaction? Could he meet the deadline? To fail would be disastrous. To be successful—after having already achieved the honor of being chosen from among several other musicians of his generation—would be an astonishing early triumph.

Although this was an important commission, it did not carry the prestige that it would have brought later in the century. Prior to this period the art of the ballet had declined to a low level not only in Russia but in the West as well. Intellectuals and musicians considered it an inferior art form, especially when compared with opera. In fact, classical ballet was thought to be unworthy of a serious composer; Tchaikovsky's *Swan Lake*, composed thirty years previously, was still a failure with the public.

Now events were rapidly moving to change this evaluation of the ballet. Diaghilev had at his disposal not only the great choreographer Michel Fokine but a number of exciting new dancers, among whom Tamara Karsavina, Anna Pavlova, and Vaslav Nijinsky were the greatest names.

Igor Stravinsky sensed that a renaissance in the ballet theater was developing and he wanted to be a part of it. He had already seen Fokine's production of *Les Dances du Prince Igor* and *Carnaval*, both of which ". . . greatly tempted me and impelled me to break through the pale and eagerly seize this opportunity of making close contact with this group of advanced and active artists of which Diaghilev was the soul."

Through the winter Stravinsky worked in close collaboration with Diaghilev, Fokine, and the set designer. Michel Fokine created the choreography for *The Fire-*

bird section by section as the music was given to him by Stravinsky—who also made sure to attend each rehearsal. Afterward the three men would adjourn to discuss its progress over a good dinner.

For the first time Stravinsky had an opportunity to observe Vaslav Nijinsky at close quarters and over a considerable period of time. (They had been introduced by Diaghilev in St. Petersburg in 1909.) Stravinsky liked the dancer's shy manner and his soft, Polish pronunciation but he was also aware of his curious mental processes. Physically, Nijinsky was extraordinary; mentally, there was something a bit disturbing about him.

Nijinsky had the face of a Russian peasant and was often silent. When he did speak, however, he gave the impression of being an uneducated youth whose intelligence had never had a chance to develop.

Nijinsky was of below-average size, with an unusually wide neck and with calf muscles that were so developed they stretched the material of his trousers taut. His features were of the Mongolian type; his fingers were stubby; and his hair, even in youth, was sparse. Jean Cocteau wrote, "You would never believe that this little monkey . . . dressed in a wide overcoat, a hat balanced on the top of his skull, was the public idol."

But he was just that—the personification of the star who seems bland and colorless offstage but radiates a magic presence once he begins to perform behind the footlights. On the stage Nijinsky's overdeveloped muscles appeared supple. He seemed much taller and moved with unforgettable masculine grace.

Offstage Nijinsky seemed childishly spoiled and im-

pulsive, and at times he could be disagreeable and ir-
ritating to work with. He was also remarkably naive.
Several years after Stravinsky met him, at a party in
London at the house of Lady Ripon, it was suggested
that the guests play a kind of parlor game during which
every member of the party was to decide what kind
of animal the others looked like.

Lady Ripon began by saying that Diaghilev looked
like a bulldog and Stravinsky like a fox. Then she said,
"Now, M. Nijinsky, what do you think I look like?"

After giving the matter some thought the famous
dancer candidly replied, "Vous, Madame—un cham-
eau" (a camel).

Nijinsky enthralled Igor Stravinsky on the stage, but
he could not teach him anything about the art of the
dance. Rather it was the famous ballet master Maestro
Cecchetti, the final authority for every step in every
ballet performed by the Russian Ballet, who taught
Stravinsky techniques of the dance with which a composer must be familiar. Although his knowledge was
limited to the classical ballet, his attitudes, which were
not dogmatic, made him invaluable as a secure anchor
for Diaghilev's sometimes erratic flights of imagination.
Cecchetti was to remain the ballet master until the
final days of the Russian Ballet, and it was he who took
the unforgettable part of the Magician in Stravinsky's
next ballet, *Pétrouchka*.

Stravinsky—now in almost daily contact with Diaghilev—soon became aware of this unusual man's enormous talents and also of his deficiencies. He was as-

tonished at the impresario's tenacity and strength of will. Once Diaghilev wanted something he let nothing stand in his way of getting it. When his objectives coincided with Stravinsky's, the composer knew he had a formidable ally. When they did not, he realized he had an equally formidable adversary.

Diaghilev seemed to be everywhere at the same time —mercurial, demanding, coaxing, exhorting, seeing little by little the emergence of the creative ideas that only others could execute. Stravinsky noted that he had a marvelous faculty for sensing at once the freshness of an idea and also of acting on the realization without pausing to reason it out. Diaghilev possessed that flash of intuitive understanding that is the hallmark of those who work successfully with creative artists.

Fokine was delighted with the Russian fairy story that Stravinsky was setting to music and worked enthusiastically on the concluding sections of the choreography. Stravinsky hoped to see Anna Pavlova given the part of the bird; her slim, angular figure seemed ideal. But Fokine and Diaghilev did not agree. The role was given to Karsavina, and once Stravinsky saw her in the part, he knew that she was perfectly cast.

But Stravinsky did not like the choreography, which appeared unnecessarily complicated. He thought the dancers had difficulty coordinating their steps and gestures with the music, "and this often led to unpleasant discordance between the movements of the dance and the imperative demands that the measure of the music imposed."

Before long, disagreements had to be forgotten or at least temporarily given a back seat. The curtain was about to go up on Igor Stravinsky's first ballet—which launched him as one of the most exciting and original composers of the twentieth century.

Any reservations Diaghilev may have felt about Stravinsky's abilities were swept away by the immediate and overwhelming success of the first performance, which was given at the Paris Opera on June 25, 1910.

Critic W. R. S. Ralston described the radiant, legendary *Zhar-Ptitsa—The Firebird*—with effusiveness typical of the period.

Its feathers ablaze with golden or silvery sheen, its eyes shine like crystal, it dwells in a golden cage. In the depths of night it flies into a garden and lights up as brilliantly as could a thousand burning fires. A single feather from its tail illuminates a dark room. It feeds upon golden apples which have the power of bestowing youth and beauty. . . .

The music of *The Firebird* is strongly reminiscent of Rimsky-Korsakov; in fact, a familiar joke among musicians has it that *The Firebird* was hatched from the nest of Rimsky-Korsakov's *Golden Cockerel.*

Although there is truth in the remark, it is only a partial truth, for the harmonies of this piece are more complex than those of Rimsky-Korsakov. There are echoes of Scriabin's middle period and of Debussy. Far more important than these influences is the vigorous presence of Stravinsky's invention—the compelling rhythms, the sense of urgency, the vibrant, shimmering orchestral color that are absolutely his own.

Diaghilev's alert, receptive ear and willingness to gamble on an untried talent had proven itself again. Prior to 1908 no one outside a few small Russian musical circles had heard the name Stravinsky. Following *The Firebird* it was known throughout Europe. Before long, an astonishing succession of triumphs were to make it known throughout the world.

6

FANTASY AND FOLKLORE

"One day, when I was finishing the last pages of *The Firebird* in St. Petersburg, I had a fleeting vision which came to me as a complete surprise, my mind at the moment being full of other things. . . ." This was how Stravinsky recalled the gestation of one of his most important works. Vividly he describes seeing ". . . in my imagination a solemn pagan rite: sage elders, seated in a circle, watched a young girl dance herself to death. They were sacrificing her to propitiate the god of spring . . . such was the theme of *Sacre du Printemps* . . . *The Rite of Spring*."

In Paris Stravinsky told Diaghilev of his idea and was encouraged to give it more thought. In the meantime Diaghilev suggested he concentrate on other projects. At the moment, Diaghilev was enjoying life in Paris a great deal; when possible he wanted his collaborators around him, and Stravinsky was one of his favorites.

The composer had easily adapted himself to life in Paris, which he now visited frequently. The French capital—although it took second place to the great German cities in musical matters—was the scene of profound changes in the arts, some of which were directly influenced by the growing prestige of the Russian Ballet.

Impressionist art, with its sensuous, enchanting, light-filled images of the world, was in its declining years and a new group of artists with the extraordinary name of Les Fauves (the Wild Beasts) was rapidly gaining ground. Their distortions and raw, vivid color were often similar to the scenery painted by the designers of the Russian Ballet. Unlike the serene paintings of Renoir, Degas, Monet, and other Impressionist masters, the art of Les Fauves was violent, intense, and only vaguely representational. They appeared to take special pleasure in flouting the middle-class proprieties with powerfully distorted canvases that, for some, seemed to exalt ugliness and sensuality.

Picasso, who had until now been occupied with the gentle, nostalgic paintings of his blue and rose periods, discovered Negro sculpture; the resultant interest in primitive art directly paralleled the interest in folk art generated by the current productions of the Russian Ballet.

Still another art movement—but one with grave implications—appeared during this period. In February 1909 a group of musicians and painters who called themselves futurists issued their first Manifesto.

In this document F. T. Marinetti, their leader, proclaimed:

The past is balm for prisoners, invalids, and men on their deathbeds who see the future closed to them. We will have none of it. We are young, strong, living—we are the FU-TURISTS. . . . We are out to glorify War—the only health-giver in the world—Militarism, Patriotism, the Destructive arm of Anarchy, Ideals that kill, Contempt for Women. It is from Italy that we launch this Manifesto of Destructive Incendiary Violence.

Since the Renaissance Italy had given the world new art forms, new civilizing institutions, new scientific discoveries. She had discovered central banking and double-entry bookkeeping and taught the rest of Europe how to do business. The wonderful commedia dell'arte had transformed the theater of the Western world. Now, through futurism, Italy nurtured totalitarian ideas that were to blossom several years later as fascism.

Mussolini was to write of the futurist Marinetti: "It is he who instilled in me the feeling of the ocean and the power of the machine."

Meanwhile, of course, few people realized the consequences these mushrooming new art movements might have. Igor Stravinsky, together with many other foreign artists working in Paris, was amused by some, baffled by others.

Later, when he began to spend more time with the futurists, he found them amusing company. One of the members of the group was the painter Giacomo Balla, who had designed the scenery for an early ballet that used the score of Stravinsky's *Fireworks*. One of the musicians associated with the group was Luigi Russolo, who gave Stravinsky a demonstration of an invention they had made that they called "the art of noises."

As he recalled the occasion in his book *Conversations with Igor Stravinsky:*

I pretended to be enthusiastic. . . . The Futurists were absurd, but sympathetically so, and they were infinitely less pretentious than some of the later movements that borrowed from them. . . . The Futurists were not the airplanes they wanted to be but they were at any rate a pack of very nice, noisy Vespas.

Paris could be wearing and, in any event, it was difficult to accomplish much work there. Stravinsky was impatient during many of these trips to return to see his growing family. Two children had been born to Catherine and Igor: a boy, Theodore, in 1907 and a girl, Ludmila, in the following year. The family had begun to spend time in Switzerland, where the fresh clean air, the frequent walks in mountain meadows glowing with buttercups and poppies quickly rejuvenated Stravinsky after busy weeks in Paris.

Igor was looking forward to beginning work on *The Rite of Spring* but first he wanted to complete an orchestral work in which the piano would play the most important part.

In composing the music [he wrote] I had in my mind a distinct picture of a puppet, suddenly endowed with life, exasperating the patience of the orchestra with diabolical cascades of arpeggios. The orchestra in turn retaliates with menacing trumpet blasts. The outcome is a terrific noise which reaches its climax and ends in a sorrowful collapse of the poor puppet.

When he finished this "bizarre" piece he took a long walk beside Lake Geneva searching for a title that would adequately express both the character of his music and the personality of the puppet. But exactly the right title was elusive until one day, after he had almost given up the search, it flashed into his mind— *Pétrouchka!* Stravinsky described him as "the eternal and unhappy hero of all fairs of all countries." He is, in fact, the Russian version of Pulcinella, one of the main characters of the old commedia dell'arte. In England he is known as Punch and in France as Polchinelle.

Not long after this momentous discovery Diaghilev came to visit the Stravinskys at the village of Clarens where they lived when in Switzerland. He had been looking forward to seeing Igor's first sketches for the *Rite,* and was prepared in his imagination for the barbaric rhythms and emotions of primitive Russia, when he was suddenly confronted with an entirely new piece —but one that immediately delighted and astonished him.

Stravinsky played the work he had just composed— which later became the second scene of *Pétrouchka*— and Diaghilev was so pleased that he urged the composer to develop the theme of the puppet's suffering and turn the orchestral piece into a complete ballet.

Together they worked out the complete story of *Pétrouchka*—developing the characters of the magician, Pétrouchka himself, his rival, the crowds, the booths, the coming to life of the dolls, and the final act, which culminates with Pétrouchka's death.

Stimulated by Diaghilev's enthusiasm and determination, Stravinsky concentrated on *Pétrouchka* and fin-

ished the score of the ballet in the village of Beaulieu,
where the family had moved when the summer was
finished.

At Christmas Diaghilev, who had returned to St.
Petersburg, wrote Stravinsky asking him to join himself, the designer Benois, and other collaborators there
so they might all review what had been accomplished
thus far. Igor immediately left for St. Petersburg, which
the severe Russian winter had covered with an unusual
amount of snow and ice. It was a busy time and, because Diaghilev was involved, an exciting one. All the
collaborators were caught up in the momentum of their
work and were much too preoccupied to consider the
political unrest that was soon to force vast changes in
Russian life.

On his return to Beaulieu, Stravinsky began the necessary revisions on the score of *Pétrouchka*, but work
was suddenly interrupted when he became ill with
nicotine poisoning and almost died. The long convalescence he was forced to endure was all the more painful because of his constant anxiety about the fate of
Pétrouchka, now definitely scheduled for a spring production in Paris.

Fortunately Stravinsky possessed an extraordinary
physical resilience and was on his feet, and at the
piano, sooner than the doctors predicted. Once again
he was on the move to see Diaghilev and discuss the
work in progress—this time to Rome, where the Russian
Ballet was giving performances at the International Exhibition.

It was in Rome that Stravinsky finished the last-minute changes in the score and that *Pétrouchka* had its first rehearsal. As usual, the composer spent a great deal of time in the theater, but whenever he was free he explored the magnificent city that he had never before visited.

"I shall always remember with particular pleasure that spring in Rome which I was seeing for the first time," he wrote, echoing the sentiments of many another visitor who is unprepared for the Mediterranean spring that suddenly brings a miraculous color and life to Italian cities that have seemed like only damp and moldering relics of the past.

Everywhere masses of golden mimosa appeared to reflect the already intense sunlight; whole streets were altered by long rows of almond trees bursting into pink blossom. Together with Benois and a Russian painter, Serov, Stravinsky visited most of the great museums and churches.

But life with the Russian Ballet was one of constant movement, and soon Stravinsky and the others found themselves in Paris. Rehearsals began at once under the direction of Pierre Monteux, a conductor in whom Stravinsky had great confidence. The dress rehearsal was held on June 13, 1911, at the Théâtre du Châtelet. The press and the elite of the artistic world were invited. Stravinsky's star had risen quickly with the presentation of *The Firebird*—now everyone waited expectantly to discover if he could write another score with the same brilliance.

The curtain rises on a vividly colored backdrop of a St. Petersburg square about the year 1830. A boisterous street carnival is in progress as a magician sets up his puppet show with three stuffed dolls—a blackamoor, a dancing girl, and Pétrouchka, a clown.

Now the magician exhibits his powers by playing the flute—a strange music that gradually brings the puppets to life. Soon they are dancing for the crowd, who are astonished and delighted by the charming spectacle. Then the scene changes abruptly to the inside of the puppet-show booth, where we see the pitiful figure of Pétrouchka being brutally beaten by the magician—a scene made even more macabre by the dancing girl, who laughs at his ugly, clumsy body, and by the blackamoor, who finally kills him.

Pétrouchka, although here presented as a highly theatrical character, is actually an old, traditional Russian figure, whom Nijinsky described as "the mythical outcast in whom is concentrated the pathos and suffering of life, one who beats his head against the wall, but always is cheated and despised and left outside alone."

More original musically than *The Firebird,* the score of *Pétrouchka* teems with new and inventive musical ideas. In it, Stravinsky makes wide use of polyrhythms, polyharmony, and polytonality. Although some of the music is influenced by Debussy's impressionism, there is still a vast difference between the Frenchman's soft, misty fluctuations of keys and chords and Stravinsky's abrupt changes.

The music of *Pétrouchka* has a sharp, staccato precision about it. Typical of this are the well-known bitonal passages in the second scene, with the arpeggios combining the keys of C major and F-sharp major. The instrumentation carries out a new concept of orchestral sonority, completely rejecting the rich blending of nineteenth-century timbres for sharp, vivid blocks of tonal color, powerful and unrelenting.

The conclusion of the work (as of most of Stravinsky's compositions) is particularly beautiful. The melancholy, dramatic ending of *Pétrouchka* recalls much of what has gone before, summing up, and leaving the audience with a moving sense of finality.

The dancing in *Pétrouchka* was no less successful than the music. Nijinsky's magnificent interpretation of the role of the puppet excited audiences and delighted Stravinsky, who believed this new role brought into play all of the dancer's genius.

Thanking Stravinsky for a copy of the score that the composer had sent him, Debussy wrote: "There is a kind of sounding magic, a mysterious transformation of mechanical into human souls, by a spell whose invention seems to be, so far, to belong only to you. . . . You will go much farther than *Pétrouchka* certainly, but you can already be proud of what this work represents."

When the work was presented in America, Olin Downes wrote: "The score is a marvel of genius, genius which creates with the certainty and the recklessness and prodigality of inspiration; which can do anything with the tonal materials employed."

The enormous success of *Pétrouchka* followed, after a relatively short time, the equally great success of *The*

Firebird. It would have been easy to understand the composer's need for a period of lying fallow, perhaps even some ineffective attempts to move in a new direction. But nothing of the sort was to happen; during these years of amazing productivity, Stravinsky was already at work on new scores—works which were to arouse even more comment and merit greater acclaim. Stravinsky was at work on the score for *The Rite of Spring.*

Igor Stravinsky at his piano

A 1917 portrait of Stravinsky by Pablo Picasso,

and a photograph taken about the same time

Picasso and Stravinsky as seen by Jean Cocteau

Sergei Diaghilev

One of Léon Bakst's designs for "The Afternoon of a Faun"

Sheet music cover designed by Picasso
for Stravinsky's "Ragtime."

Stravinsky in the Church of Santa Maria Sopra Minerva, Rome,

and strolling in the Piazza San Marco, Venice

Two views of Stravinsky conducting at a recording session.

Stravinsky and his wife, Verushka

7

"A TRAIL OF MADNESS"

Although the members of the Russian Ballet led a glamorous life that enabled them to travel widely, to meet great international artists and society figures, and to pursue their chosen profession on the highest levels, the price they paid was a heavy one. For the dancers, particularly, the constant travel and the necessity of absolute self-discipline involved a terrible nervous strain. Diaghilev sometimes said that the Russian Ballet left "a trail of madness" behind, and it was quite true that several of the best dancers had become inmates of mental institutions.

It was with a sense of relief that Stravinsky returned to Ustilug, his country estate in Russia, where he planned to devote his entire time to work on the score for *The Rite of Spring*. What better place to proceed with a work based on pagan Russia than Russia itself, in the remote countryside that Igor loved so much? Although engrossed in his work, he accepted an invitation from Diaghilev to join him at Bayreuth to hear Wagner's opera *Parsifal* in its hallowed setting. Never having seen *Parsifal* on the stage, he left with pleasure to meet Diaghilev in Germany.

As soon as they met in Bayreuth the impresario told Stravinsky that they might very well have to sleep in the open, since the hotels were filled to overflowing. Finally, and with the greatest difficulty, they found two servants' rooms. The cramped, unpleasant quarters did not help Stravinsky's frame of mind for the coming performance.

He loathed the atmosphere of the theater, even its setting and design. It reminded him of a crematorium, and he thought that undertakers might fit appropriately into the depressing background.

This solemn annual German event, with its literary and religious overtones, was precisely the kind of musical experience (if it could be called that!) Stravinsky hated. "I sat humble and motionless," he recalled, "but at the end of a quarter of an hour I could bear no more. My limbs were numb and I had to change my position. Crack! Now I had done it! My chair had made a noise which drew down on me the furious scowls of a hundred pairs of eyes." The only thought in his mind was to find a way to end this torturous experience.

Stravinsky's main objection to *Parsifal* was not Wagner's music but the pretentious religious overtones of the entire proceeding and the absurd adoration of the audience, who seemed to believe they were the observers of some profound rite.

After the pomposities of Bayreuth it was delightful to return to Ustilug, where once again Stravinsky plunged into work on *The Rite of Spring*.

As in previous years, he found the morning the most suitable time to compose. The first requisite was abso-

lute silence. He rose early and immediately after break-
fast went to his studio, where he shut the door firmly
behind him. Soulima, his son, wrote that "he composes
invariably at the piano, because, having no confidence
in abstractions as such, he needs a direct contact with
the element of sound and wishes, despite his musical
experience and memory, to subject every chord, every
interval, every phrase, to a fresh test."

Stravinsky always worked slowly and rarely composed more than two or three pages a day, often even
less. After lunch he usually attended to correspondence;
the evenings—which often lasted until the early hours
of the morning—were often spent in proofreading or
orchestration. Curiously, this work did not require Stravinsky's complete concentration but permitted him to
give some attention to other affairs. During these hours
he particularly enjoyed listening to someone read aloud.
Only when he encountered a particularly difficult problem did he ask for a short silence.

Stravinsky's ability to sustain his creative energy over
a long period was commented on by many friends and
musicians. After working and traveling with Stravinsky
for several years the violinist Samuel Dushkin wrote
that life with the composer was always stimulating,
sometimes difficult, but never boring. "His energy and
vitality are astounding and he has a power of concentration greater than that of any other person I have
ever known."

Although he worked with the usual concentration, he
was concerned about the changing status of Nijinsky
and how this would affect the new works. During con-

versations with Diaghilev in Bayreuth Stravinsky had learned that the impresario intended to assign full responsibility for the choreography of some forthcoming productions to Nijinsky. He would probably be assigned *The Rite of Spring*, but first Diaghilev wanted Nijinsky to compose "under his own strict supervision, a sort of antique tableau conjuring up the erotic gambols of a faun importuning nymphs."

Léon Bakst, who had a lifelong admiration for the classical Greek world, was assigned the sets and costumes; his knowledge was so comprehensive that he even inspired much of the choreography, showing Nijinsky gestures and stances that were characteristic of the period.

Nijinsky was completely obsessed by his role in *Afternoon of a Faun*, which became the title of Diaghilev's "antique tableau." He began to experiment with movements that were so distorted they were actually dangerous. Fortunately there were always people nearby who could catch him and revive him with warm towels, slaps, and water thrown in his face.

When unable to do as he wished, Nijinsky grew irritable and sulked. But this never interfered with his own performance, and that which he gave in *Afternoon of a Faun* was one of the most spectacular in his career. Its presentation was one of the historic moments in the history of the ballet; the sensuous, haunting score by Claude Debussy was to become a part of orchestral repertoires throughout the world.

"Nothing better could be found for this ballet than the impressionist music of Debussy," wrote Igor Stravinsky. Other musicians praised the score as well, but the choreography created a furor in the press.

French critic G. Calmett wrote: "I am persuaded that none of the readers of *Figaro* who were at the Châtelet yesterday will object if I protest against the most extraordinary exhibition which was arrogantly presented to us as a profound production. . . . We saw a faun, incontinent, vile—his gestures of erotic bestiality and heavy shamelessness."

So heated became the controversy that the Russian Embassy was drawn into the matter. The police also intervened, but permission for the ballet to continue was granted provided that Nijinsky modify one particular gesture which was considered obscene. Certainly the strain of this period helped disturb the already precarious balance of Nijinsky's psychological equilibrium. Few observers mentioned madness in their observations of him during these years; rather, he was thought of as simply a temperamental, nonverbal artist of enormous talent. Later on, events were to make him one of the most tragic artists of the era.

Meanwhile, Stravinsky was enjoying the ferment in the Parisian music world that was to be centered in the coming years upon a curious man named Erik Satie, who at the beginning of his career had aligned himself with Maurice Ravel and Claude Debussy.

When he met the latter Satie wrote:

He was full of Mussorgsky and was very deliberately seeking a way that wasn't very easy for him to find. . . . I explained to Debussy that a Frenchman had to free himself from the Wagnerian adventure which wasn't the answer to our national aspirations. . . . I also pointed out . . . we should have a music of our own—and if possible, without the *Sauerkraut*.

Satie's *Sarabandes,* written in 1887, contained harmonies typical of future Debussy works. Ravel referred to Satie's *Gymnopédies* in his *Valses Nobles et Sentimentales.* Satie, like Stravinsky, was an innovator, an explorer, and an experimenter. His germinal ideas attracted the famous Six (Louis Durey, Germaine Tailleferre, Francis Poulenc, Georges Auric, Arthur Honegger, and Darius Milhaud) and were a potent influence on other twentieth-century composers.

Erik Satie, who thought highly of Stravinsky, wrote:

To see him at a rehearsal is an excellent lesson for he knows what he wants and is keenly alive to what means of expression are at his disposal . . . the master of an amazing dynamism, he shakes the masses, waking them from their apathy. To his play with "dynamism" he brings balance and precision; above all, no pedantry. And what color in his voluntary chaos! Stravinsky shows us the whole richness of his musical power in his use of dissonance. There he finally reveals himself and intellectually inebriates us: what a marvelous magician! . . . I love and admire Stravinsky because I perceive also that he is a liberator. More than anyone else he has freed the musical thought of today, which was sadly in need of development.

German and Austrian musicians were not as receptive to Stravinsky's work. In 1912–13 Diaghilev invited the composer to accompany the Russian Ballet's tour of central Europe, where his works were to be presented for the first time. In Vienna Stravinsky was amazed at the attitude of the orchestra's musicians toward *Pétrouchka*.

I had not come across anything like it in any country [he wrote]. I admit that at that time an orchestra as conservative as that in Vienna might have failed to grasp parts of my music, but I was far from expecting that its hostility would be carried to the length of open sabotage at rehearsals and the audible utterances of such coarse remarks as *"schmützige Musik"* [dirty music].

Stravinsky was obviously unsettled by the attitude of the Viennese. One afternoon, seeing the composer's downcast features, an old workman, whose job it was to lower and raise the curtains, patted his shoulder and said, "Don't let's be downhearted. I've been here for fifty-five years, and it's not the first time that things of that sort have happened. It was just the same with *Tristan*."

In Berlin Stravinsky met Arnold Schoenberg, the Austrian composer who spoke of the "emancipation of dissonance" and who no longer adhered to the established laws of harmony. At a performance of Schoenberg's *Pierrot Lunaire,* which Stravinsky attended, a mystified audience tried to comprehend this work, which was later to be considered one of the most important compositions of the twentieth century.

Arnold Schoenberg created an entirely new organization of music that discarded the major and minor scales in favor of a method sometimes referred to as the twelve-tone system or serial music. In Schoenberg's technique, the order of the twelve pitches was fixed within a tone row. Subject to various manipulations this row, rather than traditional melody and harmony, became the basis of the composition, thus producing music that lacked the familiar tonality previously taken for granted.

Igor Stravinsky—who was to write serial music himself forty years later—did not at this time have an interest in Schoenberg's theories. "I did not feel the slightest enthusiasm about the esthetics of the work," he wrote unequivocally.

When the central European tour was over Stravinsky once again returned to finishing the orchestration for *The Rite of Spring*, while rehearsals continued in Paris. Whenever he attended these, and he did this frequently, misunderstandings and disagreements with Nijinsky seemed unavoidable.

The dancer was struggling to achieve a great work but his marvelous talents appeared to lie solely in the performing arts, not the creative. Stravinsky had seen this long ago, of course, but was unable to do anything about it except try to control his impatience when dealing with Nijinsky—and often with Diaghilev as well. The moment was coming close when the opening-night curtain would rise on *The Rite of Spring*.

8

A RIOT IN PARIS

Igor Stravinsky's brilliant ballet scores were following one another in quick succession. Although Diaghilev and the others involved in the production of *The Rite of Spring* were fully justified in believing that still another success was in the making it is unlikely that anyone realized one of the great events in musical history was about to take place.

Rehearsals proceeded with the usual temperamental flare-ups and disagreements that characterized the workings of the Russian Ballet. The most disturbing problem, as far as Stravinsky was concerned, was the fact that Nijinsky had been named choreographer.

Although Stravinsky realized the man was an incomparable dancer and mime, he was also aware of the fact that he was ignorant of the most elementary notions of music and could neither read music nor play any instrument. He thought that Nijinsky's response to music was expressed "in the most banal platitudes."

There were many reasons why Nijinsky had been given this assignment, and there was little chance that Diaghilev would change his mind. Michel Fokine—

who had proved an invaluable mainstay during the early years of the Russian Ballet—had finally broken with Diaghilev and left the company. Two other choreographers were busy with assignments. But overruling all considerations was Sergei Diaghilev's great attachment for the young dancer, his desire to develop Nijinsky's latent abilities and bring him ever greater acclaim.

From the first Nijinsky began to demand a fantastic number of rehearsals, for reasons that were never clear to Stravinsky. Each one was a trial to the composer, who found that because Nijinsky knew nothing about music, it was impossible to convey his ideas to him.

For Igor it became an increasingly exasperating experience that demanded enormous patience and tact. Nijinsky's thought moved slowly and relied heavily on grasping situations (and dealing with them) on an intuitive level. Stravinsky's thought processes were swift and easily conveyed by his articulate speech. The results of such a confrontation can easily be imagined.

One stormy scene led to another, and nothing was helped by the fact that Diaghilev moved quickly to protect Nijinsky from criticism. Sergei Lifar, a young dancer who witnessed many of these scenes, wrote: "Had Stravinsky, one wonders, any notion of why Nijinsky had become so difficult to work with? Did he know that Diaghilev, in the privacy of his room, demonstrated every step to Nijinsky, which explains why he was forced to turn deaf ears to every criticism and maintain and defend a creation not his own but Diaghilev's?"

Problems multiplied, disputes sputtered and flared, and bursts of temper became the order of the day. Yet finally, miraculously, *The Rite of Spring* was ready for its premiere performance on February 4, 1913.

The Rite of Spring is in two parts. The first is called "The Adoration of the Earth," and its sections—without pauses between them—depict the Harbingers of Spring, Dances of the Adolescent Boys and Girls, a Mock Abduction, Spring Rounds, Games of the Rival Tribes, a Procession of the Tribal Sages, and Dance of the Earth.

Part II is entitled "The Sacrifice." After its introduction depicting the Pagan Night the following sections describe the Mysterious Circles of the Adolescents, Glorification of the Chosen One, the Evocation and Ritual of the Ancestors, and finally the Chosen One's Dance of Death.

The general effect is a violent, unprecedentedly savage portrayal of pre-Christian Russia so dissonant and shocking that it enraged the first audiences who heard and saw it. No one was prepared for the obscene gestures, the powerful evocation of sweating, bestial, primitive man.

But how much did this famous first-night audience really see and hear? Stravinsky himself did not stay to witness the chaos that erupted "at the first bars of the prelude, which at once evoked derisive laughter . . . these demonstrations, at first isolated, soon became general, provoking counter-demonstrations and very quickly developing into a terrific uproar."

He fled backstage, where he remained at Nijinsky's side. Nijinsky was not dancing on this occasion but was standing on a chair screaming, ". . . sixteen, seventeen, eighteen . . ."—measured beats that helped the dancers to keep time.

It is doubtful that anyone could hear very much except the growing uproar in the theater. Stravinsky held Nijinsky by his clothes, for the dancer was furious and ready to dash onto the stage, where he might impulsively do something that would further outrage the audience. Meanwhile, Diaghilev, distracted but attempting to keep his composure, kept ordering the electrician to turn the lights on and off, hoping in that way to put a stop to the noise.

The theater shook with a violent mixture of applause, catcalls, and a general uproar that Paris had not witnessed since the production of *Hernani,* a tragedy by Victor Hugo that caused rioting between the romantics and classicists of 1830.

The Amercan writer Carl Van Vechten recalled:

A certain part of the audience was thrilled by what it considered a blasphemous attempt to destroy music as an art and, swept away with wrath, began very soon after the rise of the curtain, to make catcalls and to offer audible suggestions as to how the performance should proceed. The orchestra played unheard, except occasionally, when a slight lull occurred. The young man seated behind me in the box stood up during the course of the ballet to enable himself to see more clearly. The intense excitement under which he was laboring betrayed itself presently when he began to beat rhythmically on the top of my head with his fists. My emotion was so great that I did not feel the blows for some time.

Insults flew through the air; people whistled, shouted, and laughed. The conductor, Pierre Monteux, kept throwing desperate glances toward Diaghilev, who was trying to sit calmly in his box while making signs that Monteux should keep the orchestra playing.

Finally, when the lights had to be turned on, people in the audience actually began to fight with each other. One beautifully dressed lady in an orchestra box stood up and slapped the face of a young man who was hissing in the next box. Another pro-Stravinsky society woman spat in the face of one of the demonstrators.

At this point Diaghilev, now standing in his box, shouted, "Je vous en prie, laissez achever le spectacle!" (Please, let us finish the performance), and the pandemonium temporarily quieted down. Backstage, the noise and confusion seemed as bad as it was in the auditorium; the dancers were trembling, some almost crying. Others could not even return to their dressing rooms but remained in the wings, astonished and helpless.

Finally, the end of the performance came and the curtain rang down on what had been one of the most tempestuous theatrical performances of the twentieth century. Diaghilev, who usually guarded Nijinsky's dressing-room door from celebrity seekers, was not able to stem the tide on this night. Soon the small room was filled with people who spilled out into the hall, excitedly discussing, explaining, and condemning the events of the evening. It was a scene of disorder and backstage drama sure to warm the heart of any balletomane.

Whatever the general public might think of *The Rite of Spring*, most musicians seemed united in their belief that this was a tradition-breaking work that would one day find wide acceptance. Diaghilev, Stravinsky, and the other collaborators were glad to hear words of encouragement, but finally the strain of the evening began to tell. Longing for fresh air and quiet, Stravinsky, Diaghilev, Nijinsky, and Jean Cocteau slipped out of the theater and hailed a cab. They told the driver to take them to the Bois de Boulogne, the great park near the outskirts of Paris. Among the several versions of this drive, Cocteau's is the most poetic.

For a long time the foursome were quiet as they drove through the cool night air. The night was fragrant with the smell of acacias and other flowering trees; the ponds placid and sparkling in the moonlight. After a while Diaghilev began mumbling in Russian. Cocteau wrote, "I could feel Stravinsky and Nijinsky listening attentively and as the coachman lighted his lantern I saw tears running down the impresario's cheeks. He went on mumbling slowly.

" 'What is it?' Cocteau asked.

" 'Pushkin.' "

Then there was a long silence, after which Diaghilev spoke, and, as Cocteau wrote, ". . . the emotion of my other companions seemed to be so keen I could not resist interrupting to find out why.

" 'It is difficult to translate,' said Stravinsky, 'really difficult and too Russian . . . much too Russian. . . . It is something like "What do you say to a jaunt to the islands?" Yes, that's it. It is very Russian you see, because at home we go to the islands the way we are going to the Bois de Boulogne this evening, and it was while we were going to the islands that the idea for *Le Sacre du Printemps* came to us.' "

"It was the first time that the riotous evening had been referred to," Cocteau recalled. "You can't imagine the gentle nostalgia of these men and no matter what Diaghilev may have done later I shall never forget his great tear-stained face as he recited Pushkin that night in the Bois de Boulogne."

When the first reviews were in, it became clear at once that most of the critics' outrage was directed at the music, which the French critic Rambert called "intensely refined Hottentot," a music that was characterized by "ear-splitting intolerable discords, and ponderous, imperious rhythms. . . ."

Cocteau, more interested in its literary than its purely musical character, described *The Rite of Spring* as a symphony "impregnated with wild pathos, with earth in the throes of birth." He also referred to "the noises of farm and camp, the little melodies that come to us out of the depths of the centuries, the panting of cattle, profound convulsions of nature."

Debussy, writing to Stravinsky to thank him for an inscribed copy of the score, said: "It is not necessary to tell you of the joy I had to see my name associated with a very beautiful thing that in the passage of time will be more beautiful still. For me, who descends the other slope of the hill but keeps, however, an intense passion for music, for me it is a special satisfaction to tell you how much you have enlarged the boundaries of the permissible in the empire of sound."

Yet many years later, when Debussy's letters were published, it became known that he had another view of *The Rite of Spring*.

To Ernest Ansèrmet he wrote, "You know how much

I admire *Pétrouchka,* but the *Rite* disturbs me. It seems to me that Stravinsky is trying to make music with non-musical means, just as the Germans apparently pretended to be able to make beefsteaks out of sawdust."

Later on, in a more vicious mood, he wrote to another friend that Stravinsky was "a spoilt child who sometimes cocks a snook at music. He's also a young barbarian who wears flashy ties and treads on women's toes as he kisses their hands. As an old man he'll be unsupportable—that's to say, he won't support any other music; but for the moment he's unprecedented."

When Stravinsky became aware of what seemed to be Debussy's two-faced attitude he wrote with astonishment, "Was it duplicity, or was he annoyed at his incapability to digest the music of the *Rite* when the younger generation enthusiastically voted for it?"

Another important French composer defended this work without reservations. It was gratifying to Stravinsky when ". . . my friend Maurice Ravel intervened practically alone to set matters straight. He was able to see, and he said, that the novelty of the *Rite* consisted, not in the 'writing,' not in the orchestration, not in the technical apparatus of the work, but in the musical entity. I was made," Stravinsky concludes, "a revolutionary in spite of myself."

What was this extraordinary music that outraged the public and upset the critics? Sixty years later musicologists throughout the world are agreed that *The Rite of Spring* marked an important breakthrough in musical history. It signaled the direction composers must take; it banished nineteenth-century romanticism.

Like a thunderbolt *The Rite of Spring* announced the forthcoming admission of the brutal, primitive side of man that had been tactfully swept under the carpet during the Victorian and Edwardian periods. The *Rite* was the musical counterpart of the new exploration of the irrational by psychologists, graphic artists, and such contemporary writers as Marcel Proust and James Joyce.

In this work Stravinsky relied heavily on the national idioms of Russia—themes and folk melodies that he often directly reproduced or adapted. But it was in the rhythm—a new kind of rhythm entirely—that Stravinsky created first and foremost fresh and original work. Of this piece American composer Aaron Copland wrote: "Heading the list of Stravinsky's original gifts was his rhythmic virtuosity. Nothing like it had ever been heard in Paris . . . it was Stravinsky who revitalized our rhythmic sense. He gave European music what amounted to a rhythmic hypodermic. It has never been the same since."

This rhythm is made of units of time that are too short to be called beats. They are even too short to be indicated individually by the conductor's baton. Musicologist Charles Demuth writes that "these units . . . are quite strictly equal to each other. A pair of them forms a reasonably brisk beat or three of them together form a moderate beat, still not slow. The two kinds of beats occur in no simple pattern, but so as to defy expectation, and their irregularity is insisted upon by strong staccato accents."

Another Stravinsky innovation is beats that are often

marked by a thud in the accompaniment. Stravinsky's rhythms have some resemblance to jazz but their great power derives from their astonishing energy and a quality of relentless momentum.

The distinctive rhythm of *The Rite of Spring* is so new, so powerful, so hard to master, and so fascinating that it attracts students as an abstract problem unrelated to the melody and harmony of the music.

French musicians Olivier Messiaen and Pierre Boulez have both published enthusiastic commentaries on it. Boulez especially gives it the highest praise. Some students claim that the *Rite* represents a sort of emancipation of rhythm comparable to Schoenberg's emancipation of dissonance; they maintain that the rhythm in Stravinsky's music works independently of melody and harmony, or at least that it subordinates melody and harmony to its elemental power.

Diaghilev referred to the *Rite* as "the twentieth century's Ninth Symphony." Cocteau said, "Stravinsky was the first to teach me how to insult habits, without which art stagnates and remains a game." Everyone who was interested in the arts talked about *The Rite of Spring,* and they are still talking about it. It is one of the most important musical works of the twentieth century.

By April 1914 concert performances of the work were being given without dancing or scenery to distract the audience. People were no longer hissing and stamping their feet but applauding enthusiastically. Stravinsky, who had returned to Russia, followed the various performances and their reception with great interest, but there was an atmosphere of anxiety in St. Petersburg that made it difficult to think of musical matters. Stravinsky remained at home briefly and was soon prepared to leave for Switzerland.

On my way from Russia [he wrote], via Warsaw, Berlin, and Basle, I was very conscious of the tense atmosphere all over central Europe and I felt certain that we were on the evening of serious events. A fortnight later war was declared. As I had been exempted from military service, there was no need for me to return to Russia which, though I had no inkling of it, I was never to see again as I had known it.

9

REFUGE IN SWITZERLAND

Cut off from Russia by the war, Stravinsky suffered through many periods of apprehension for relatives and friends who remained behind. Often in his reading he returned to the Russian folk poems that had interested him for so many years.

"What fascinated me in this verse," he wrote, "was not so much the stories, which were often crude, or the pictures and metaphors, always so deliciously unexpected, as the sequence of the words and syllables and the cadences they create which produces an effect on one's sensibilities very closely akin to that of music."

The Russian folktales continued to occupy Stravinsky's thoughts during this period, and often after he left his reading chair or desk the bright, haunting images remained in his mind. After a busy morning of work Stravinsky would often walk in the brisk, cold air of the hills surrounding Geneva. The clarity of the air in the winter, the purity and beauty of the deep snows were exhilarating. The nearby villages were clean and prosperous-looking. There was no doubt about it—if one had to be an exile, the Swiss mountains were an excellent place.

The Stravinskys decided to spend the winter of 1914 in Clarens, where they remained after the declaration of war. It was an especially difficult time for Catherine, who was now pregnant with her fourth and last child, to be named Maria Milena. (A second son, Soulima, had been born in 1910.)

Very soon Catherine and Igor became aware of the difficulties that besiege the exile in wartime. They were entirely dependent upon financial resources in Russia, which were becoming increasingly harder to obtain; soon they began to feel genuine deprivation.

Diaghilev, who had taken refuge in Florence, was also experiencing a difficult time both financially and emotionally. The war had upset all his plans for new tours of the Russian Ballet, and with his entrepreneurial energies bottled up, he became more erratic and difficult than ever. Although part of the company was already dispersed, he continued to carry on as best he could, trying to maintain morale and explore what possibilities remained open.

Visiting Diaghilev in Florence, Stravinsky was shocked by the depths of his depression and the general disorder and apprehension that was spreading throughout Italy. The country was totally unprepared to enter a war for which the people had no enthusiasm.

Later in the year Stravinsky visited Diaghilev in Rome, where the impresario had taken an apartment for the winter; immediately it became a magnet for Russian artists living in western Europe. Among many others, Stravinsky saw Sergei Prokofiev there.

It was clear to all of these men that no matter what

course the war took in Russia, chaotic conditions would remain for a long time. Revolution had been in the air for too long, and they knew that sooner or later it would remake Russia. No one knew how this would affect the lives of her artists; the one certainty was that working conditions would be extremely difficult.

Fortunately, most of these men had traveled widely in western Europe; most spoke French and often some other languages as well. Relocation would not be as painful as it might have been for those who had never been outside Russia. Still, they were all aware that Russia as they had known and loved her was about to vanish and that a new Russia was coming into being. Many of them would never be able to find their place in the new order of things.

Back in Switzerland Stravinsky found that his wife's health had deteriorated; hoping to find more comfortable quarters for her, the family moved to the Hotel Châteaux d'Oex, but there was no place in these cramped quarters where Stravinsky could work. His rapidly diminishing funds made it impossible for him to take a proper studio anywhere.

Finally, as a last desperate resort, Stravinsky asked a music dealer to allow him the use of a storage room full of empty Suchard Chocolate packing cases. Apparently it was a kind of shed, and it opened out into a little chicken run. Optimistic and determined as usual, Stravinsky moved in a small upright piano, new and out of tune—and began to order his thoughts.

He tried to work through sheer force of willpower,

but the room was so cold that the piano strings broke. He had them fixed, tried for two days to work in an overcoat, fur cap, and snow boots with a rug over his knees, but finally realized that it was humanly impossible to continue this way.

Just then someone told him of a spacious, warm room in the village home of a couple who were at work most of the day and would be glad to rent it for a modest fee. Stravinsky had hardly moved in all of his things when once again he found working conditions almost totally unsatisfactory, because of the family's loud and uncontrollable emotional outbursts whenever they were present.

Once again the Stravinskys returned to Clarens, while they searched the area around Lausanne in the hope of finding a suitable place where they could remain for the duration of the war. Eventually they discovered the tiny village of Morges, on the banks of Lake Geneva, where they were to spend five years.

C. F. Ramuz, the Swiss novelist and friend of Stravinsky's, recalls how the Swiss women, sewing in the open air not far from Stravinsky's window, would nod as they heard the strange musical sounds. "It is the Russian gentleman," they announced to newcomers. The curious music could now be heard every morning, for Stravinsky finally had the good working conditions that he found essential.

Visitors to his various studios were always interested in learning of his orderly work habits and seeing the neat organization of his possessions. They were also impressed by his invention and thrift, for he did not use the specially printed music paper with staves but had a plain notebook on which he printed the staves with a special metal wheel he designed himself.

Stravinsky commented many times on the creative process, and here, as in his attitude toward the nature of music itself, his thinking was devoid of any romantic ideas. Writing of creativity, he said: "This appetite that is aroused in me at the mere thought of putting in order musical elements that have attracted my attention is not at all a fortuitous thing like inspiration, but as habitual and periodic, if not as constant, as a natural need."

And yet, aware of the mysterious element of creativity, he also wrote: "The study of the creative process is an extremely delicate one. It is impossible to observe the inner working of this process from the outside. It is futile to follow its successive phases in someone else's work. It is likewise very difficult to observe it in one's self."

He also said, "Inspiration comes with working just as appetite comes with eating," which confirms the many observations by those who have seen him at work. Stravinsky's self-discipline and concentration are legendary.

It was in Stravinsky's studio in Morges that Diaghilev —who in 1915 took a nearby villa—heard the first two scenes of *Les Noces* (The Wedding).

The impresario was so moved that he burst into tears, saying this work would certainly prove to be the most beautiful and "the most purely Russian creation of the Russian Ballet." Remembering this encouragement and enthusiasm in what was a very difficult period, Stravinsky dedicated the work to Sergei Diaghilev.

Although Stravinsky was to work many years on the score of *Les Noces,* the first rush of inspiration was, as usual, vivid and intense. *Les Noces* is one of Stravinsky's most passionate works.

The composer had never seen a Russian peasant wedding. In any event, he was certainly not interested in a literal description of such a ritual and celebration but wanted ". . . to use as I liked those ritualistic elements so abundantly provided by village customs which had been established for centuries in the celebration of Russian marriages. I took my inspiration from these customs but reserved to myself the right to use them with absolute freedom."

Stravinsky had no intention of using the traditional orchestra; his first plan was a huge orchestra, even larger than that required by *The Rite of Spring*. There would be two main categories of sound: wind (including voices) and percussion. The wind section would include the choir, woodwinds, and brasses; the other section would make use of two string orchestras, but one playing only pizzicato and the other with the bow. After much experimentation Stravinsky finally realized that this scheme, which would have required about 150 players, was unworkable and gave it up.

Another attempt to solve the problem was the division of instruments into groups, keeping the groups separate on the stage. After discarding this idea he conceived another that would make use of an electrically driven mechanical piano and harmonium, an ensemble of percussion instruments, and two cimbaloms. (The cimbalom, a stringed instrument, is the national instrument of Hungary.)

Eventually this possibility was also ruled out because of the difficulty of finding expert cimbalom players and synchronizing the mechanical elements with the singers and the nonmechanical instruments.

While continuing to wrestle with the problems presented by *Les Noces,* Stravinsky turned to other ideas and plans for future work. Both work and life seemed to move very slowly now. Scarcity of money made it essential to find relaxation in the simplest things, such as walking and talking with friends who were in the same predicament. Often the conversation turned to the nature of music, on which the composer has written with extraordinary insight and perception.

"The phenomenon of music," he said once,

is given to us with the sole purpose of establishing an order in things, including, and particularly, the coordination between man and time. To be put into practice, its indispensable and single requirement is construction. Construction once complete, this order has been attained, and there is nothing more to be said. It would be futile to look for, or expect anything else from it. It is precisely this construction, this achieved order, which produces in us a unique emotion having nothing in common with our ordinary sensations and our response to the impressions of daily life. One could not better define the sensation produced by music than by saying that it is identical with that evoked by contemplation of the interplay of architectural forms. Goethe thoroughly understood that when he called architecture petrified music.

Many similar thoughts were recorded later when Stravinsky's several books were produced. But it was now, in Switzerland, during these long years of exile and seclusion, that Stravinsky was able to brood on the mysteries of creativity and esthetics. Nevertheless, confinement of any kind could only be frustrating for Stravinsky's soaring creative spirit. He looked forward to Diaghilev's return from America and the inevitable excitement that he generated wherever he went.

10

COMPOSER IN EXILE

When Stravinsky finally received word of the impresario's arrival in Spain, in the early spring of 1916, he at once went to join Diaghilev in Madrid. Instead of showing the immediate effusiveness with which artists of the Russian Ballet generally greeted each other, Diaghilev looked Stravinsky sorrowfully in the eye as he said, "I have been waiting for you like a brother. . . ."

Pale and weary, he launched into a long account of the trials he had had to endure on the Atlantic crossing. He had been in a state of constant apprehension, since the munitions ship he was traveling on was forced to change course continually in order to avoid the German submarines.

Igor listened sympathetically, and after copious glasses of tea were drunk—Russian style, with lemon —Diaghilev and Stravinsky toured the city. It was Stravinsky's first visit to Spain, and he had become fascinated by it as soon as his train crossed the frontier. "At the very boundary the smell of frying in oil became perceptible," he wrote. "When I reached Madrid at nine o'clock in the morning I found the whole town still fast asleep and I was received at my hotel by the night watchman with lantern in hand." Spring was in the air; the Spaniards were staying up even later than usual and, consequently, sleeping later than usual.

All the little characteristics of the Spaniards' daily life pleased me immensely, and I experienced and savored them with great gusto. They struck me as marking a vivid change from the monotony of the impressions generally received in passing from one European country to another, for the countries of Europe differ far less among themselves than all of them together do from this land on the edge of our continent where already one is in touch with Africa.

Stravinsky was greatly impressed by Toledo and by the Escorial—a magnificent complex of palaces, museums, and religious buildings about twenty-five miles from Madrid. He believed that these two short excursions taught him far more about the country than a vast amount of reading historical treatises could have done.

My glimpses of these two places evoked in me visions not so much of the horrors of the Inquisition or the cruelties of the days of tyranny as a revelation of the profoundly religious temperament of the people and the mystic fervor of their Catholicism, so closely akin in its essentials to the religious feeling and spirit of Russia.

After spending many hours discussing future projects for the Russian Ballet, Stravinsky returned to Morges, where he remained until autumn. It was a quiet time for Stravinsky but one of increasing anxiety. By now it was perfectly clear to everyone that the war would not be short. Although one was probably more secure in Switzerland than anywhere else in Europe, money was still needed to support daily life, and funds were decreasing. Stravinsky's journals are full of his financial problems at this point (and yet, whenever it became necessary to see Diaghilev, somehow or other he managed to find the wherewithal).

In the spring of 1917, Stravinsky returned to Rome, where Diaghilev had once again taken an apartment, and where he was surrounded by the usual glittering array of talent. Léon Bakst was there, as were the great conductor Ernest Ansermet, Jean Cocteau, and Pablo Picasso.

Diaghilev, who had planned a special performance of the Russian Ballet for the benefit of the International Red Cross, suddenly realized that it was no longer appropriate to play *God Save the Czar*, since the monarch had recently abdicated. This work, which was traditionally played before all Russian gala performances, had to be replaced with something else.

Deciding to substitute the famous "Volga Boatmen's Song" instead, Diaghilev asked Stravinsky to write the instrumentation for the full orchestra. As it was necessary to complete the job in one night, Stravinsky dictated the score, chord by chord, note by note, to Ernest Ansermet, who copied it and had it ready to rehearse the next morning.

Afterward Diaghilev gave a great reception in the Grand Hotel, at which there was also an exhibition of cubist and futurist painters, whose depictions of squares, rectangles, and abstracted machines were gaining favor. The whole troupe then proceeded to Naples and more performances; in this city the one thing that attracted Stravinsky and Picasso more than anything else was the famous aquarium.

When the performances were over Stravinsky boarded the train for Switzerland, eagerly anticipating his return to the peace and quiet of Morges. In his luggage was a portrait of himself that Picasso had drawn in Rome. After packing it away he had forgotten about it, and at the frontier town of Chiasso, where the authorities make a routine check of passports and luggage, was amazed when they began to examine the drawing with unusual curiosity.

Everyone in the railway compartment was silent as the officers spent several minutes poring over what they seemed to consider a mysterious design, talking in hushed voices in the corridor, and then returning for a further examination. At last they confronted Stravinsky with their findings. The drawing was not a portrait at all but a mysterious document that undoubtedly contained secret information.

"Nothing in the world would induce them to let it pass," Stravinsky said. "They asked me what it represented, and when I told them that it was my portrait, drawn by a distinguished artist, they utterly refused to believe me. 'It is not a portrait—but a plan!' they insisted."

"Yes," Stravinsky agreed, "the plan of my face but of nothing else."

This was a time of war, and the soldiers, aware that they could take no chances, refused to accept Stravinsky's explanation of the strange drawing. They did allow him to send it to Lord Berner, the British ambassador in Rome. Having cleared it with the Italian authorities, Lord Berner later forwarded the picture to Stravinsky in Paris by diplomatic pouch. The only real loss was one of time; the frontier officials had deliberated so long that Stravinsky missed his connection and was forced to spend the night in Chiasso.

By the end of 1917 Stravinsky found himself in one of the most difficult periods of his life. The communist revolution had just triumphed in Russia, and it deprived him of the last resources that had from time to time been trickling through to him in Switzerland. His financial situation was no longer just serious but acute and becoming more desperate with each passing day.

Nor were there any friends to whom Stravinsky might turn for help; all of them were in similar, or even worse, circumstances. They became so obsessed by the need for money that their conversation—when they met at the local cafe—continuously returned to their main preoccupation: money and how to get it.

Eventually they found themselves grasping wildly at a variety of bizarre schemes. After a few days had passed and the group had time to examine these schemes carefully, it realized they were hopeless. Still, the friends often met to search for some means of escape from their alarming situation. It was during these talks that Stravinsky and the writer Ramuz developed the idea of creating a little traveling theater, one which would be easy to transport from place to place and could be used in even the smallest villages. The scenery would be of the simplest kind and could easily be set up and dismantled in any hall or building or, when the occasion arose, even in the open air.

Stravinsky, who seemed stimulated by the very restrictions of this scheme, insisted that the work be very simple. He envisioned a production that would require only two or three characters and a small number of instrumentalists. This was an imaginative scheme, beset with many problems and difficulties, yet the only one, thus far, that seemed at all reasonable.

Soon Ramuz and Stravinsky were discussing their scheme with Ansermet, who was to be the orchestra leader, and with René Auberjonois, whose province was to be the decor and costumes. Even the exact itinerary was planned out. The main stumbling block—as always for artists about to embark on an ambitious project— was finding a wealthy patron or group who could be persuaded to underwrite the scheme.

Several refusals depressed the artists, who were easily downcast at this difficult time. Then, buoyed by Stravinsky's absolute determination, the group finally met Werner Reinhart of Winterthur, a well-known patron of the arts who promised to finance their production.

Stravinsky immediately turned to Aleksandr Afanasiev's famous collection of Russian folktales, which had never been far from his desk during these years of exile. Before long Stravinsky and his collaborator Ramuz had settled on a cycle of legends dealing with the adventures of a soldier who, having deserted the army, is confronted by the devil. The conflict between them provides the main action of the piece.

Many of these stories had come into being during the cruel period of enforced recruitment under Czar Nicholas I. A group of songs of that time, called *Rekroutskia,* also expressed the sorrows of women and girls who had lost their sons and lovers.

With his usual understanding of what was timely, of themes that were in the air, Stravinsky realized that these stories, although specifically Russian, created an atmosphere and called up emotions now being experienced by millions of people in a world at war. For this reason the collaborators decided to adapt the Russian tales to the present time and to eliminate their purely Russian character.

The time had come also for Stravinsky to make the many decisions about the technical aspect of the new work. The question of the choreography, if there was to be any, or how much, was yet to be resolved. It would certainly be minimal. One way or another, Stravinsky reasoned, the orchestra must be in full view on the stage:

I have always had a horror of listening to music with my eyes shut . . . with nothing for them to do. The sight of the gestures and movements of the various parts of the body producing the music is fundamentally necessary if it is to be grasped in all its fullness . . . those who maintain that they only enjoy music to the full with their eyes shut do not hear better than when they have them open, but the absence of visual distractions enables them to hear the reveries induced by the lullaby of its sounds and this is really what they prefer to the music itself.

Because of the mobility necessary for this new production it was obvious that Stravinsky would have to be content with a very restricted orchestra. He knew that the easiest solution would be the use of some polyphonic instrument such as the piano or the harmonium, but both of these were ruled out from the start.

The harmonium was eliminated chiefly because it does not possess accents and is therefore limited in the range of tonal color. The piano was not used because it might have appeared that the composer's financial resources were restricted—an impression he wanted to avoid if possible. But the most important reason he chose not to use the piano was his fear that its part in the production would become too important; the audience would be distracted by the virtuosity of the pianist.

The instruments on which Stravinsky finally decided were the most representative types, in treble and bass, of the instrumental families. For stringed instruments he chose the violin and the double bass; for the woodwinds, the clarinet, "because it has the biggest compass," and also the bassoon. The brasses were represented by the trumpet and trombone; the percussion was played by only one musician.

Stravinsky and his collaborators worked on *Histoire du Soldat* until the early part of 1918. Although they were hoping to produce it in the summer, it was not until September 18, 1918, that this historic work was given its first performance at the Lausanne Theater.

The curtain rises on a rustic, stylized setting of woods, a stream, and a village in the distance. The soldier, returning to his village after a leave from the army, meets the devil by the banks of the stream. Disguised as an old man, the devil carries a butterfly net and conveys an attitude of harmlessness. In exchange for a book of magic, he gets the soldier's fiddle and also persuades the young man to spend three days of his leave with him.

Occasionally the actors speak dialogue; sometimes they simply mime the action. (At first the narrator or reader was intended as the main figure on the stage but one who did not himself participate in the action. Later on it was decided that from time to time he should intervene in the action.)

A miraculous element enters the next scene when the soldier, having finally reached his village, discovers that he has been away not three days but three years. Once again the devil comes on the scene, this time disguised as a cattle merchant. He shows the soldier how the magic book can help him to gain a fortune.

In the next scene (of which there are six) the soldier has achieved wealth but is now tired of it. Dressed as an old woman who sells old clothes, the devil appears. Among his articles for sale is the soldier's fiddle, which he at once wants to reclaim and to play again. Finding that he cannot bring any sound from it, the soldier hurls it away and destroys the book of magic.

The soldier, now having lost his wealth, arrives at a town where the king has promised his daughter's hand to anyone who can cure her of her illness. The devil, disguised as a virtuoso violinist, invites the soldier to a game of cards; they play and drink until the devil falls unconscious and the soldier takes possession of the fiddle.

In the next scene the soldier plays his fiddle for the princess. The music enchants her; she rises and dances to the rhythms of a tango, a waltz, and a ragtime tune. At the end she and the soldier embrace but they are interrupted by the devil, who now appears in his true guise, with pointed ears and forked tail.

By his extraordinary playing the soldier renders the devil helpless, and with the aid of the princess he drags his body offstage. But the devil is not yet defeated. In the last scene the soldier and princess, now married, are approaching the soldier's village for a visit when once again the young man falls into the power of the devil, who has regained control of the fiddle. Irresistibly attracted to the music, the soldier deserts the princess and follows the devil.

Histoire du Soldat is a prime example of Stravinsky's particular brand of eclecticism. It satirizes the common music of the dance hall; it is reminiscent—in parts—of a vaudeville show; and yet it immediately brings to mind the terse precision of an eighteenth-century chamber work. Stravinsky has given each of the seven instruments virtuoso passages; each asserts its individuality and then merges into the whole.

As in so many Stravinsky works to come, *Histoire du Soldat* blended the classic with the contemporary and realistic. It is a fascinating, pungent work that is ranked as one of his most important achievements.

11

A BACKWARD LOOK

On November 11, 1918, World War I came to an end; what had seemed an endless nightmare was finally over. Until the morning of the following day, in London, Paris, New York, and thousands of other cities throughout Europe and America, crowds of people sang and danced in the squares and streets.

Meanwhile, as the populations of war-torn countries looked forward to years of peace, the ideological forces of left and right fought for control. The German kaiser was in flight; in Bavaria the Communists had seized power; and Hungary had fallen under control of the Communist leader Béla Kun. In Russia, amid scenes of great desolation and poverty, the young Communist government struggled to survive.

But the Allies and other countries of western Europe had had more than enough of bloodshed and brutality; in their determination to enjoy the fruits of victory, they could disregard the continuing struggles of central and eastern Europe. People felt an urgent need to play again, to laugh and be silly, to delight in life and art and nature. As soon as possible, those who could afford it made plans to go abroad again.

For Russian refugees marooned in Switzerland the immediate future appeared difficult and uncertain. The Peace of Brest-Litovsk, negotiated by Russia and Germany without the Allies, had placed all Russian exiles in an awkward position; they were regarded as undesirable immigrants, and innumerable difficulties were placed in their way when they wished to travel.

After a long convalescence from influenza, Stravinsky tried to put worries about his future out of his mind by returning to *The Firebird* once again—this time to arrange it as a suite for a smaller orchestra than required by the original score. The composer changed many parts entirely, cut others, and eventually succeeded in reducing the number of musicians needed to about sixty.

This was important work but still a kind of marking time for Stravinsky, who seemed to be at the height of his powers during these years. Although he had enjoyed several years of being close to his growing family, Stravinsky was nervously frustrated by his long exile in Switzerland. He was eager to be at work again on some project of larger dimensions and to collaborate with other artists. As soon as possible he left for Paris, where Diaghilev was forming plans to take the entire company of the Russian Ballet to London.

Diaghilev was visibly cheered by the armistice and full of ideas about the glorious future of the Russian Ballet. Stravinsky, delighted to see Diaghilev more like his old self, soon launched into a detailed and enthusiastic description of the success of *Histoire du Soldat* and the pleasure he had taken in its creation.

As he spoke, Diaghilev listened with unconcealed boredom. Stravinsky was not surprised because he remembered only too well that the great impresario was incredibly jealous about his friends and collaborators. He obstinately refused to recognize their right to work on projects in which he had no part. He saw such undertakings as a breach of faith or outright desertion.

Less understandable was the realization that Diaghilev even found it difficult to tolerate Stravinsky's appearance as a conductor or pianist of his own works. It was tiresome for Stravinsky to have to deal with such extraordinary egomania, and only the passage of years helped him to understand the nature of Diaghilev's serious emotional problems.

Many years later Stravinsky wrote:

Now that he is dead, it all seems rather touching, and it has left no trace of bitterness; but when I tried during his lifetime to get him to share my enjoyment of successes which I had made without his participation, and encountered only his obvious indifference, or even hostility, it hurt me; I was repelled and I suffered acutely.

Diaghilev only expressed interest in the conversation when it turned to a discussion of Stravinsky's new projects for the Russian Ballet. He began to speak enthusiastically about staging the opera Stravinsky had been working on for several years—*The Nightingale*. Diaghilev promised that Léonide Massine would be assigned the choreography, and Henri Matisse the decor and costumes.

Stravinsky was tempted to work with such excellent

artists but he was convinced that *The Nightingale* should be performed on a stage without dancing, and he declined Diaghilev's offer.

The impresario thought quietly for a time, reviewing projects that he hoped would interest Stravinsky. One of his ballets, *The Good-Humored Ladies,* with music by the eighteenth-century Italian Domenico Scarlatti, had been very successful and he was considering the possibility of another work set in this time and based on the music of another Italian composer.

While in Italy, he had made a thorough search for unpublished eighteenth-century manuscripts at the various Italian conservatories; copies of these were augmented by further discoveries in English libraries. Diaghilev showed some of his findings—predominantly works by Pergolesi—to Stravinsky; he suggested that the composer study them and, if he felt stimulated by the material, adapt them for a new ballet.

In particular Diaghilev drew Stravinsky's attention to a manuscript dated 1700, which he had found in Naples. It contained many of the comic exploits of *Pulcinella,* the Italian version of *Pétrouchka.* One episode in particular appealed to both men.

It was the story of some Neapolitan girls who have fallen in love with the roguish Pulcinella. The young men to whom they are betrothed are mad with jealousy and plot to kill him. After a series of exploits involving the disguises and mistaken identities of which the commedia dell'arte was so fond, the marriages finally take place, including that of Pulcinella.

Stravinsky was very attracted to this idea. The compositions of Pergolesi, he said, he "liked and admired immensely . . . I have always been charmed by Pergolesi's Neapolitan music, so entirely of the people and yet so exotic in its Spanish character." (Much Neapolitan art was influenced by the long Spanish occupation of that city.)

Nevertheless, Stravinsky, who was well aware of the problems involved, wrote that "it was a delicate task to breathe new life into scattered fragments and to create a whole from the isolated pages of a musician for whom I felt a special liking and tenderness."

But this was not a major problem, and after returning to Morges and starting to compose the new score for *Pulcinella,* Stravinsky found that the work gave him great pleasure. The study of Pergolesi's scores, although most were only fragmentary sketches or outlines, increased his respect for this eighteenth-century composer.

Once again—perhaps remembering his success with *Histoire du Soldat*—Stravinsky decided to use a small orchestra. Of course this time it was a true approximation of the eighteenth-century orchestra as it had actually existed. For this reason, there were to be no percussion instruments. Finally, Stravinsky decided that the three singers would form a part of the orchestra and not be identifiable with any of the characters on the stage.

Soon Stravinsky was traveling back and forth from Morges to Paris more regularly than ever before, caught up in the spiraling excitement and activity that often marked the creation of new works for the Russian Ballet. Massine, the choreographer, as usual had begun to work from a piano arrangement of the score sent to him piece by piece as Stravinsky completed it.

Exhilarated by the progress of the work, Stravinsky wrote, "*Pulcinella* is one of those productions—and they are rare—where everything harmonizes, where all the elements—subject, music, dancing, and artistic setting—form a coherent whole."

He thought Massine's work one of his greatest creations. He also liked Picasso's contribution, but Diaghilev was horrified when the artist showed him Offenbach-period costumes with side-whiskered faces instead of masks. He had been hoping for designs in the style of the old Italian commedia dell'arte and became so enraged that he gave way to one of his temperamental fits. He threw the drawings on the floor, stamped on them, and abruptly left the room, slamming the door behind him.

Picasso was deeply offended but he agreed to have another go at it. He produced a new setting, showing an eighteenth-century theater with its rococo boxes, which overlooked—as a kind of framework—the smaller scene where the action of the ballet would take place. In the final version, this theatrical framework was also scrapped and only the Neapolitan scene remained: the familiar Italian stucco apartment houses on moonlit streets, with a glimpse of the Bay of Naples and Mt. Vesuvius in the background.

Many years after the premiere of this work Stravinsky said that *Pulcinella* was his discovery of the past—not

literally of course, but as a backward look that revealed
how the past might be made to nourish the work of
the present. Yet this work shocked a good many people. They could not appreciate it on its own merits,
nor could they understand it as a part of the meta-
morphosis Stravinsky's creativity was about to undergo.
Many simply believed that he had renounced his true
Russian heritage, that he had deserted contemporary
music in order to exploit the classics. Dogmatic minds
viewed such an effort as sacrilegious; they could not
conceive of how a new work so inextricably bound with
an older one might still function as an integral and successful whole.

Pulcinella has the stylistic qualities of the eighteenth
century, its forms and elegance, but they are freshly
seen and masterfully resketched through Stravinsky's
genius. It is a key work in the study of his art.

The score of *Pulcinella* marked a definite turning
point in Stravinsky's career, which was, in part, determined by the political events that had drastically
changed Russia. After the Bolshevist Revolution the
country remained in turmoil; cultural affairs of necessity took second place after the great work of recon-
structing the devastated Russian economy. Consequently factory workers, not artists, were the important
men of the period.

It was clear that Stravinsky's future lay in the West,
but certainly not in Switzerland, comfortable and safe
haven though it may have been during the war years.
Although Stravinsky had created some of his greatest
works during this period, it had been a time of uncer-

tainty. A fresh start in a new direction had to be taken.

During the postwar years most artists found the choice of residence an easy one. There was only one city that could offer them a unique cultural atmosphere that mysteriously seemed to arouse the creativity of those who remained there. Although the words are rarely used now, in those days if you spoke of the "City of Light," your listener knew at once that you were referring to Paris.

12

YEARS OF TRAVEL, YEARS OF WORK

Nowhere was the preeminence of Paris more apparent than in the world of music. Germany had maintained her leadership in musical affairs before World War I despite the rise of the French Impressionists, led by Debussy and Ravel. After the war Paris became a haven for many great composers and thus also attracted thousands of music students, who were delighted to be able to pursue their studies in France rather than Germany.

Now too, startling developments in the graphic arts were taking place, the most sensational being that of Dada, the "anti-art" movement which had begun in Zurich and Munich during the war years. Art critic John Canaday has written, "Dada in its origins was not so much an art movement as it was an anti-art eruption in which poets and artists, in a combination of high spirits and despair, danced a jig in the international graveyard created by World War I." Society— so it seemed to the young people of this time—had played a dirty trick on them; they were determined to respond as outrageously as possible.

Tristan Tzara, the leader of Dada, said, "We spit on

humanity . . . Dada is the abolition of all logic . . . there is great negative work to be done. We must sweep everything away and sweep clean." A German advocate of this movement stated, "Dada was shock-treatment for a crazed humanity . . . since the age aims at the destruction of all that is noblest and best in life, the Dadaist courts the absurd, loves every kind of disguise, game, or deception." In the streets adherents to the new creed carried placards reading "Dada kicks you in the behind and you like it!" The word itself, meaning "hobby-horse," had been chosen at random from a dictionary by those who wished to underscore the meaninglessness of life by giving a meaningless name to a meaningless art movement.

The dominating theme of Dada was its absolute irreverence for established norms and beliefs. This was displayed by combinations of materials and forms that seemed to have no natural relationship with each other.

Sometimes strange dances were performed, charades of people oddly dressed and strangely similar to the "happenings" of the 1960's. "Junk music" of accidental sounds, poems of nonsense, or simultaneously declaimed in several languages or imaginary languages, were solemnly performed at Dadaist centers throughout Europe.

Detractors of Dada saw this as a purely sensational bid for attention on an infantile level. How much of it was genuinely felt? Was it a sincere expression of despair at the years of horror through which the world had just passed? The many frauds such a movement attracts make a fair evaluation difficult. But now that Dada can be studied from the distance of a few decades it does appear to have been a meaningful esthetic expression of the times.

Dada was only a part of the cultural ferment of Paris in the 1920's. Throughout the city artists, writers, and musicians were engaged in producing important works. Even many of the hotels and restaurants were decorated by a riot of huge flattened flowers and bold patterns inspired by the paintings of Henri Matisse.

Ernest Hemingway was writing the first of his famous novels, and James Joyce was about to publish *Ulysses,* a book that horrified many people even more than the Dadaist nonsense exhibited as art in the galleries along the Rue de Seine. With so much activity going on it was inconceivable that the Stravinskys would choose anywhere but Paris; in 1929 they made preparation to move to this city, where, as Igor Stravinsky wrote, "at the moment, the pulse of the world was throbbing most strongly."

First the family left for Brittany, where they planned to spend the summer months. The beaches and fresh sea air might be fine for the children, but Stravinsky, who could not share their enthusiasm for this part of France, wrote to his friend Ramuz in Switzerland:

I can't say I like Brittany very much—not as I liked the country in the canton of Vaud.

In the first place, the weather's always bad; and then, for my part, I don't find the place at all French. . . . It's true the peasants are good fellows; but that's so everywhere. . . . I'm bored by the "picturesque" and everyone spends their time strolling up and down the streets of this

village of fishermen. The place is full of conventional middle-class trippers, who can't afford to go to Deauville. It's
not at all amusing—people who start singing outside our
windows when we're in bed, and louder than is necessary
in the streets at night . . . I'm sleeping badly and composing music.

Returning to Paris, Stravinsky found the city still
summerlike. Along the grand boulevards the great
plane trees were still heavy with the dust of summer;
in the evening they imparted a topaz color to the lights
—still partly served by gas at this period—that illumi-
nated the streets. Then, swiftly, a sudden cold wave
sent the crisp leaves swirling along the sidewalks and
into the streets. Autumn had come, and with it, a new
and busy schedule for Stravinsky.

Diaghilev was busy planning a new performance of
The Rite of Spring but was facing serious financial difficulties because his assets were still frozen in Russia.
Gabrielle Chanel, one of the great French couturieres
of the time, came to his assistance, not only lending
him financial aid but going so far as to have all the
new costumes executed in her dressmaking shops.

One of the most important events of the season was
a revival of the ballet *Parade* (first produced in 1917)
—the joint effort of Jean Cocteau, Erik Satie, and Picasso, and considered by many to be one of the most important productions of the twentieth century. Igor Stravinsky delighted in its originality. It confirmed his
admiration for Satie's talent and the strong creative
force he exerted in French musical affairs.

The Stravinskys spent the autumn of 1920 at Gabrielle Chanel's house at Garches, near Paris. They were also there in the winter of 1921, presumably because finances did not permit the family to move directly into Paris. Apparently the situation did not improve, because when they left Chanel's house it was once again for the Atlantic coast, this time the village of Anglet near Biarritz.

As things were turning out, although "the throbbing pulse of the world" might be beating most strongly in Paris, the Stravinskys would not be moving there. At least not the family; Igor was often to be in Paris while wife and children remained on the seacoast. Biarritz became a place for the composer to work, to refresh himself, and to be with his family. But there wasn't a great deal of time left for family matters during these hectic years.

Throughout these years the Russian Ballet often rehearsed in Monte Carlo, the tiny principality in the south of France that had become a haven for Russian exiles. Even before the war it was popular with Russian aristocrats; the luxury in which they lived was legendary. Now fewer remained, but still one might easily run into the Grand Duke Dmitri (who had planned the murder of the infamous monk, Rasputin) or the Grand Duchess Anastasia, wearing a flaxen wig and sitting in the bar of the Hôtel de Paris.

Stravinsky's mother had come to live with her son and his family in France, and there seems to have been a fresh outburst of personality clashes. Mme. Stravinsky, as strong and stubborn as ever, would never bow to her son's equally strong will. Nor did she approve of his music.

A friend, meeting her in Paris at a performance of *The Rite of Spring,* asked (knowing that Mme. Stravinsky was familiar with the work only from records): "Are you thrilled to hear *The Rite* at last in a concert hall?"

"Je pense que ça ne sera pas de la musique pour moi" (I don't think it will be music, for me), she answered emphatically.

But her reservations were not shared by growing numbers of people who every year were coming to acknowledge Stravinsky's international prestige. People not only wanted to listen to his music and watch his ballets but, if at all possible, to meet him, to enhance the prestige of their parties and receptions with his presence.

One of the most impressive and most memorable of such gatherings was a large summer party given by Mr. Schiff, a wealthy American, at the luxurious Hotel Majestic. This man had set his heart on bringing together the four men he considered the greatest living artists: Pablo Picasso, James Joyce, Marcel Proust, and Igor Stravinsky.

Both Picasso and Stravinsky joined the festivities early, but midnight came and went and there was still no sign of Joyce or Proust. After a while the Irish writer appeared, specter-like and apparently quite ill.

He was given a chair near his host and sat there with his head between his hands and a glass of champagne in front of him.

It wasn't until three o'clock that the legendary Marcel Proust appeared, pale and ghostly, dressed as always in black evening clothes and white kid gloves. The author of *Remembrance of Things Past* was shown to a chair on his host's left, where he found himself sitting next to Stravinsky. After a preliminary exchange of remarks he said, "Doubtless you admire Beethoven."

"I detest Beethoven," Stravinsky grumbled.

"But, cher maître (dear master), surely those late sonatas and quartets—?"

"Pires que les autres" (Worse than the others), growled Stravinsky.

Ernest Ansermet intervened in an attempt to maintain peace and, as the group fumbled to begin a new conversation, James Joyce began to snore.

Many years later Stravinsky said that his remark about Beethoven was made because of the cult-like worship that surrounded this composer, one which had little to do with a true understanding or appreciation of his music.

Since Stravinsky had held to a long-standing unromantic view of what music can communicate in terms of human emotions and ideas, he was naturally impatient with the "noble expressions" some people claim to hear in music.

Furthermore, he had no respect for those who were especially awed only by works of the past; such people, he claimed, were not really having a genuine esthetic experience but simply paying homage to an embellishment of their own self-image and social status. Stravinsky believed that no one who is truly receptive to any art can ignore the present, "for it is only those who are essentially alive who can discover the real life of those who are dead."

And once again Stravinsky was about to test those who were "essentially alive."

13

LES NOCES

Diaghilev often talked of *Les Noces*—begun in 1914 but never produced, mainly because Stravinsky had never been able to resolve the instrumental problems to his satisfaction. In 1921, when Diaghilev heard Stravinsky's latest solutions for the remaining problems, he felt that at last the composer was on the right track and urged him to complete the instrumentation. Exerting the famous Diaghilev willpower, he definitely scheduled the first performance of *Les Noces* for the 1923 season of the Russian Ballet.

Although his initial ideas about *Les Noces* had proved unworkable, Stravinsky had no intention of compromising his conception of the unique form he insisted upon. Now, reflecting on past experiences, he saw that *Histoire du Soldat* had taught him a good deal and also led in the direction he must go to complete *Les Noces* successfully.

Histoire du Soldat—which had placed the instrumental players side by side with the actors and dancers on the stage—had been a very successful production. Because of his satisfaction with this work, Stravinsky wanted to place the orchestra for *Les Noces* on the stage. He was not at all disturbed by the apparent incongruity that might be felt when the musicians were seen to be in evening dress while the dancers wore costumes of a Russian character.

As was to be expected, the very mention of *Histoire du Soldat* infuriated Diaghilev and made him more determined that his production of *Les Noces* would be executed only as he saw fit; certainly it would have no connection with that other production, which had been created without him.

No efforts to convince Diaghilev were of any use, so finally, but with reluctance, Stravinsky agreed to submit to the impresario's more traditional idea of the staging. However, the instrumentation was entirely a matter for Stravinsky to decide. He had long ago altered his original conception of the work and no longer considered using the mechanical pianos or the unusually large orchestra. The final solution was unique and typically Stravinsky-like. The ensemble called for a four-part chorus with four soloists (soprano, mezzo-soprano, tenor, bass) and an unusual orchestra that consisted of four pianos, xylophone, timpani, a bell, four drums, tambourine, bass drum, cymbals, and triangle.

Stravinsky attended every rehearsal of *Les Noces*—not just as a spectator but irresistibly drawn to the production of this extraordinary work. At first he would indicate roughly what he had in mind, but soon, thoroughly aroused, he would take off his coat and sit down at the piano. Then he began singing and playing, emphasizing the dramatic elements he thought essential for a successful production. Often he would go on in this way until he was completely exhausted. By that time new life would have been infused into the rehearsal, and the whole company would start again with renewed vigor and inspiration.

Meanwhile Diaghilev was busy with the decor and costumes. Nathalie Goncharova, who had been given this assignment first, produced elaborate but realistic designs that were not at all what he had in mind. Alternating between gentle persuasion and imperative demands, he prevailed upon her to simplify them to an almost severe austerity.

The first dress rehearsal was held in the Princess de Polignac's Paris house with Stravinsky conducting. Diaghilev, Nijinsky, other leading artists of the Russian Ballet, and members of the Paris intelligentsia assembled in the audience for what was soon recognized as another Stravinsky triumph.

The general effect of his libretto is a kind of vivid abstraction that does not concern itself with any literal details but communicates the vigor of a peasant wedding. There is no characterization in the usual sense of the word, since Stravinsky refused to identify any particular character with any particular singer. Nevertheless, the words generate a strong response in the listener —partly, perhaps, because of their unadorned simplicity.

> Dear Heart, dear Wife, my own,
> Dearest treasure, my sweet, my honey,

Fairest flower, let us live in happiness
So that all men may envy us.

Toward the end, with a rustic naiveté, the libretto continues,

Hear the Bridegroom saying
"I would sleep now,"
And the Bride replying
"Take me with you."
Hear the Bridegroom saying
"Is the bed narrow?"
And the Bride replying
"Not too narrow."

Part One of *Les Noces* shows the preparations for a peasant wedding at the bride's house, where her hair is ceremonially plaited. Then the action moves to the groom's house, where the young man receives the blessing of his mother and father and the ritually lamenting mothers and consoling friends are heard as the procession leaves for the feast. At the traditional "red table" there is drinking and joking in sight of the nuptial bed, which must first be warmed up by a couple who are already married. We are caught up in the joy and exultation of the wedding feast, after which the door is closed on the bedroom and the guests listen to the groom's solemn song to the bride.

In *Les Noces* Stravinsky used only one folk melody; although the remainder of the material is purely his own melodic invention, the composer succeeded in creating a work that some Russian critics have called "the most perfect evocation of genuine Russian folk life and folk music."

Victor Belayev, the Russian musicologist, has written that virtually all the melodic material is developed from a single thematic germ that is stated in the opening measures. The relationship of the singers to the orchestra is highly individual and unusual. For the most part, the voices carry the main theme, and they are responsible for creating a sense of tonality. The orchestra sustains the rhythm and harmony—the latter usually in a different tonality from that of the voices. The resulting dissonances are even more pronounced than those of *The Rite of Spring*.

A mood of excited anticipation was felt by those who were invited to the dress rehearsal of *Les Noces* at the Princess de Polignac's Paris house. The dancer Serge Lifar recalls:

I sat on the floor, absorbing the music and rhythms, and floating away, as it were, into the inner world of this ballet. The powerful sounds enthralled me, swept me on, thrilled me with their mystery, their timelessness, and illimitable space, their wild Russian upsurge. Both body and soul seemed as though shattered by the Russian dance tunes, the sad music of the ritual folk songs sent a pang through the heart, and the church bells of mysterious old Asiatic Russia sounded preternaturally familiar and moving.

Vladimir Dukelsky—better known as Vernon Duke, composer of "April in Paris"—was another member of the audience who recorded his impressions of this important event. He was struck by the beauty of

the black and white decor . . . the choreography shrewdly
mixing paganism and geometry, and best of all, the lumin-
ous, "undressed," uncannily persuasive music, the four pianos
clashing and clicking their teeth, the constantly changing
rhythms chasing each other without stopping breathing, fired
my whole being. At the final curtain I screamed "Bravos"
with the rest of the Stravinskyites. . . .

This enthusiasm was seconded by the audience at the
first-night performance, which was an even more gala
occasion. After the premiere, two of Stravinsky's American friends, Gerald and Sara Murphy, gave a large
party on a converted barge moored in the Seine—a
festive, elegant event of the type that had long ago become a commonplace experience for Igor Stravinsky.

Yet he was anything but casual about the details of
such parties. Although this one was scheduled to begin
at seven Stravinsky arrived a little earlier to inspect the
dining room and make sure that the seating arrange-
ments of the guests were satisfactory to him. His own
seat, in the place of honor on the right of the Princess
Edmonde de Polignac, was left unchanged, but others
were rearranged.

Soon the many artists, musicians, writers, and society
people began to arrive, among whom were Picasso,
Cocteau, Darius Milhaud, Ernest Ansermet, Diaghilev,
and many of the beautiful young dancers of the Russian
Ballet.

After a long dinner, interspersed with music provided
by Ansermet at the piano, Jean Cocteau—whose sense
of the theatrical rarely deserted him—put on the barge
captain's uniform and went around the barge with a
lantern as he put his head through portholes to an-

nounce "On coule! On coule!" (The ship is sinking! The ship is sinking!)

The high point of the evening came when Ernest Ansermet took down from the ceiling a huge laurel wreath bearing the inscription *"Les Noces—Hommages."* He held it for Stravinsky, who dashed the length of the room and artfully jumped through the center, to the amusement of the applauding guests.

Many critics who had come to appreciate the dissonances in Stravinsky's earlier work were hostile to those they discovered in *Les Noces.* In England especially reviewers responded with such hostility that the great English writer H. G. Wells felt impelled to write to the London *Times*:

I have been very much astonished at the reception of *Les Noces* by several of the leading London critics. . . . Writing as an old-fashioned popular writer, not at all of the highbrow sect, I feel bound to bear my witness to the other side. I do not know of any other ballet so interesting, so amusing, so fresh, or nearly so exciting as *Les Noces.* I want to see it again and again. . . . The ballet is a rendering in sound and vision of the peasant soul, in its gravity, in its deliberate and simple-minded intricacy, in its subtly varied rhythms, in its deep undercurrents of excitement, that will astonish and delight every intelligent man or woman who goes to see it. . . .

Although it was undoubtedly the most important work of the decade *Les Noces* never achieved the wide popularity of Stravinsky's other theater pieces—possibly because it is one of the most strident works in modern music. The insistent, overpowering rhythms in the score are difficult for the average theatergoer to accept. When these are understood as the expression of urgency and passion, the dynamic originality of *Les Noces* becomes clearer.

After *Les Noces* the composer's interest in folklore and peasant life was finished, at least as far as his own creative efforts were concerned; never again would he produce works whose use of vibrant Russian folk drama enthralled thousands of listeners. For many it was the concluding piece of a period in which he produced his finest works.

14

A STRAVINSKY
TURNABOUT: THE
NEOCLASSIC PERIOD

Les Noces was more than the crowning success of Stravinsky's long and brilliant career with the Russian Ballet; it was also to be the last score that he would ever write specifically for Diaghilev's company, and it marked, at least temporarily, his loss of interest in the theater.

It seems clear that one factor contributing to Stravinsky's thoughts about leaving the theater was his renewed interest in religion. Sergei Lifar writes, "In 1923 we find him finally repudiating the ballet, his religious conviction no longer permitting him to employ his art in anything so base as the theatrical ballet . . . . " In a letter never released for publication Stravinsky spoke of the ballet as "l'anathème du Christ."

Igor Stravinsky was born and baptized in the Russian Orthodox Church, but when he was seventeen or eighteen he refused to participate in religious rituals of any kind. Now the iconoclastic years of youth had passed. Fame and a degree of material success had come with extraordinary speed, and yet, as so often happens when early recognition is achieved, Stravinsky may have felt a surfeit of worldly pleasures and rewards.

The composer never said very much about this transitional period in his life, but it is known that the year 1924—after the family left Biarritz and moved to 167 Boulevard Carnet, Nice—marked a profound change in his life. It was in Nice that Stravinsky met Father Nicolas, a Russian Orthodox priest who ". . . was practically a member of our household during a period of five years . . . . " In 1926 Igor Stravinsky rejoined the church and became a communicant for the first time since 1910.

It was during this year that the first of several religious experiences occurred which were to have enduring effects. Stravinsky was returning to Nice on his first airplane flight. En route from Venice he stopped in Padua to join a group of pilgrims celebrating the seven hundredth anniversary of St. Anthony.

"I happened to enter the Basilica," Stravinsky wrote many years later, "just as the Saint's body was exhibited. I saw the coffin, I knelt, and I prayed. I asked that a sign of recognition be given when and if my prayer was answered, and as it was answered, and with the sign, I do not hesitate to call that moment of recognition the most real in my life."

This experience provided the inspiration for the first of his religious works, the "Pater Noster" for mixed choir a cappella, not published until 1932.

Another significant incident took place in Nice before

the composer was to leave for a trip to Venice, where he was to perform his piano sonata.

He had been having trouble with an infected finger that refused to heal. The usual remedies being of no help, he went to pray in a little church near Nice, before an old icon that was reputed to possess miraculous powers. Although a believer, his faith must have faltered, since he believed there was a good chance the concert would have to be canceled. Because the finger was still festering when he walked onto the stage of the Teatro La Fenice, he first spoke to the audience and apologized for what he suspected was going to be a poor performance.

Then he sat down, removed the little bandage, and discovered that the finger was—miraculously, so it seemed—completely healed. This experience deepened Stravinsky's faith, and more than once after that time he affirmed, "I do, of course, believe in a system beyond Nature."

Stopping briefly in Genoa during these years, Stravinsky spent part of an afternoon browsing through a bookshop where he came across a life of St. Francis of Assisi. He bought the book, read it through that night, and later said that it was this experience which inspired his conception of *Oedipus Rex*. What particularly impressed him was the discovery that St. Francis spoke French (which he knew imperfectly) whenever he wished to express some profound or solemn thought. Following such a lead, Stravinsky reasoned that Latin, rather than a language he knew, would enable him to impart a monumental and timeless character to the work.

Using an ancient tongue further appealed to Stravinsky because he had been unable to resolve the language problems of his future works. "Russian, the exiled language of my heart, had become musically impracticable, and French, German, and Italian were temperamentally alien . . . ."

After some deliberation, Stravinsky decided to compose an opera-oratorio based on the *Oedipus Rex* of Sophocles, and he set about looking for a librettist. The choice was not a difficult one because the composer had not long before seen Jean Cocteau's *Antigone,* a theatrical production for which he had the greatest admiration. It was precisely Cocteau's subtle and haunting development of the ancient myth in modern guise that Stravinsky hoped he would bring to bear on *Oedipus Rex.*

In the course of several conversations between the two men the work gradually took shape, but the initial conception remained unaltered. From the beginning Stravinsky was convinced that he wanted not an action drama but a "still life." Yet he underscored the need, when outlining his ideas to Cocteau, of a conventional libretto with arias and recitatives.

Meanwhile Stravinsky's career had taken on a completely new aspect—that of performer. Time which in earlier years had been devoted to the Russian Ballet was now given to a variety of new projects. The ballet company itself had changed drastically; Diaghilev was often ill or depressed. Nijinsky, now hopelessly insane, was confined to an institution in Switzerland, where he was to die, still mad, in 1950.

During the 1920's and 1930's Stravinsky was frequently on tour both as a conductor and a pianist. Early in 1925 he made his first visit to America and was greeted, upon arrival in New York, by the usual mob of journalists who appeared when he arrived in a foreign country. When asked what he thought of modern music he replied, "I detest it!"

"But you, maestro—" another journalist protested with bewilderment.

"I don't write modern music," Stravinsky replied without a moment's hesitation. "I only write good music."

American audiences were familiar with Stravinsky's music and flocked to see him in the roles of pianist and conductor. He considered the tour a great success and apparently made a favorable impression on Mrs. Elizabeth Sprague Coolidge, a great patron of music. The following year she commissioned him to write a thirty-minute ballet score for a festival of contemporary music to be held at the Library of Congress, Washington, D.C. Diaghilev, already distressed at Stravinsky's loss of interest in the Russian Ballet, became infuriated at what he considered an outright defection to the Americans. His only comment was, "Cette Américaine est complètement sourde" (This American lady is completely deaf).

Stravinsky, ever practical in monetary matters, immediately answered, "Elle est sourde, mais elle paye" (She is deaf, but she pays).

"Tu pense toujours à l'argent" (You always think of money), Diaghilev acidly replied. It was a sentiment echoed many years later by Robert Craft, the young conductor who was to become Stravinsky's indispensable assistant. Craft suggested that the initials I. S. would be more truly representative of Igor Stravinsky if the position of the *I* were superimposed on the *S* to suggest the symbol of the dollar.

As a theme for the Coolidge commission Stravinsky, continuing his exploration of classical themes, chose Apollo, leader of the muses. Because of the brevity of the work he reduced these to three—Calliope, Polyhynmnia, and Terpsichore—poetry, mime and dance.

While planning work on *Apollo* the collaboration with Jean Cocteau on *Oedipus Rex* continued. Much to his delight, Stravinsky found that Cocteau was more than patient with his criticisms. The whole book was rewritten twice, and even after that he submitted it to a final shearing.

The finished libretto of *Oedipus Rex* arrived just after New Year's Day of 1925. Stravinsky, who had been awaiting it eagerly, plunged into work on the score. He was delighted with the final version: " . . . all my expectations from Cocteau were justified. I could not have wished for a more perfect text or one that better suited my requirements."

One of the first problems Stravinsky encountered was

his difficulty in working with the Latin text. Although he had studied this language at school he feared that he had forgotten almost all of it—but, as often happens with languages, it only appeared that he had forgotten it. Knowledge of the language gradually returned as he studied and worked with the text. Soon the events and characters of the great tragedy came to life, and Stravinsky, exhilarated by the challenges and even the problems of this new work, found the music rapidly taking form.

He felt an extraordinary freedom, a sense of liberation in using this unfamiliar tongue and the ancient themes that are so remote from the modern world. It was an unexpected joy to compose music to the Latin language, which he felt almost imposed a majestic dignity on the work. He said he no longer felt dominated by the phrase, by the literal meaning of the words. Consequently the sounds of the words assumed a new importance.

Both Cocteau and Stravinsky tried to keep their work on *Oedipus Rex* as secret as possible; it was to be a surprise for Diaghilev, who would be celebrating the twentieth anniversary of his theatrical activities in the spring of 1927. One wonders what was in the minds of the collaborators, who were only too well aware of the impresario's attitude toward productions of his associates that did not involve him. Yet his very absence seemed to spur on Cocteau and Stravinsky. Working with great concentration, Stravinsky finished the score of *Oedipus Rex* on March 14, 1927.

At the premiere in Paris a somber stage set provided the scenic background; the chorus remained stationary as in the Greek drama, and several singers appeared in costumes and masks but moved only their heads and arms. The reader, in modern evening dress and speaking in modern French, delivered short explanatory notes on the plot.

Since the music of *Oedipus* is constructed mainly along the lines of an eighteenth-century oratorio, the first reactions were that it was an evocation of the style of Handel. This was a superficial appraisal, since the sources Stravinsky used are far more varied. Listening carefully, one can easily detect suggestions of ancient church chant or plainsong, and even references to nineteenth-century Italian opera—in short, eclecticism as only Stravinsky could practice it.

After the premiere Diaghilev, as was to be expected, remarked that *Oedipus Rex* was "un cadeau très macabre" (a very macabre gift). He said little more about this ambitious production that had been created without him and could, therefore, have little merit. There were other, more profound reasons for Diaghilev's attitude toward *Oedipus Rex* and also for the deepening sense of depression and tragedy that surrounded him during these years.

Oedipus Rex, a production without dancing, and in Latin, was a marked departure from the works Diaghilev had produced. It seemed a leap toward the future, in which the great impresario's role was most uncertain.

For years his health had been declining, and it was weakened further by the fact that, though a diabetic, he refused to take insulin regularly.

The vicissitudes of life with the Russian Ballet, the constant traveling, the famous feuds, the loss of his estates and fortune in Russia had become too heavy a burden to carry. Hadn't Diaghilev himself commented on the trail of madness that the Russian Ballet left behind because of its arduous and frenetic life? He had escaped madness, but a long series of neurotic crises had seriously damaged his physical well-being.

During the final years of Diaghilev's life his relations with Stravinsky deteriorated badly. With the passage of time Stravinsky found Diaghilev's temperamental and jealous nature no easier to endure; on the contrary his outbursts of rage became more and more difficult to take with equilibrium. Matters were not helped by Diaghilev's realization that both he and the Russian Ballet were in their declining years. Consequently he sought modernism at any price to cloak his ever-present fear of not being in the vanguard. "The search for something sensational; uncertainty as to what line to take—these things wrapped Diaghilev in a morbid atmosphere of painful gropings," Stravinsky wrote.

More and more Stravinsky found himself evading Diaghilev's questions and trying as tactfully as possible to avoid arguments that could not possibly be resolved.

The last time Stravinsky saw Diaghilev was from a distance on the platform of the Gare du Nord railway station in Paris, where both were taking the train for London. Their relations had reached such a low point that neither made an attempt to speak to the other.

Six weeks later Stravinsky was at Echarvines near the lake of Annecy in eastern France, where the family had gone to spend the summer. Hearing that Prokofiev was living nearby, Stravinsky went to pay him a visit with his sons and stayed very late. When they returned home Stravinsky found his wife waiting patiently in her robe; she had sat up late to give him the news of Diaghilev's death, which had just been telegraphed from Venice.

Stravinsky was not shocked at the news because he was aware of the impresario's struggle with diabetes. This in itself would not have been so crucial considering Diaghilev's strong constitution, but recent reports about his declining health from mutual friends had disturbed Stravinsky, who feared that the end was near.

Diaghilev was mourned by thousands of people; his name is often found in journals and memoirs written by his contemporaries, and he is credited with being one of the most imaginative and visionary theatrical producers the world has known. Recalling memories of Diaghilev in his autobiography (published in 1936), Stravinsky wrote:

At the beginning of my career he was the first to single me out for encouragement, and he gave me real and valuable assistance. Not only did he like my music and believe in my development, but he did his utmost to make the public appreciate me. He was genuinely attracted to what I was then writing, and it gave him real pleasure to produce my work, and indeed, to force it on the more rebellious of my listeners, as for example, in the case of *Sacre du Printemps.*

. . . It is only today, with the passing of the years, that one begins to realize everywhere and in everything what a terrible void was created by the disappearance of this colossal figure, whose greatness can only be measured fully by the fact that it is impossible to replace him. . . .

Diaghilev's death occurred in 1929, a year that marked the end of an era—not only for the Russian Ballet but for the entire world.

15

M. IGOR FEDOROVICH STRAVINSKY, CITIZEN OF FRANCE

Few people realized at the time of the American stock market crash in 1929 that its effects would be so widespread or that such vast numbers of people throughout the world would suffer extreme deprivation. But during the 1930's, as always in times of economic hardship, Parisians returned to money-saving devices that they, more than most people, seem to understand so well.

One began to see curious pairs of furry mittens in the windows of apothecary shops. They were the work of the resourceful poor of Paris, who when times were very bad would sometimes steal cats and fatten them up for a time. After the cats were killed they served a twofold purpose; they provided food and their skins could be sold as mittens. It was a disagreeable way to exist, but when there were few choices even this became possible.

Most of the Russian emigrés had been accustomed to reduced circumstances since their flight from Russia. Consequently the onset of the depression did not force major changes on their lives. They lived in the vicinity of the Russian church in the Rue Daru, where they lent an exotic note to the drab Parisian quarter. Actually it was like a small Russian city with Russian cafes, bookshops, jewelry and antique stores, and intimate bars. Stravinsky recalled that "during the feast days the hubbub and decor were like an oriental fair."

During the twenties and early thirties the church and the area surrounding it were a focus of social life for all Russians living in Paris, whether they were members of the Russian Orthodox Church or not. Toward the end of the decade, because problems within the church could not be resolved, many little churches sprang up all over Paris, some of them "portable and pocket-sized," housed in apartments, studios, or wherever sufficient space could be found. In the Rue d'Odessa one was located over a small nightclub. Stravinsky wrote later: "I remember when money had to be raised to buy a half hour of quiet during the Saturday night Easter service and until midnight, when, as soon as the priest had cried, 'Christos Voskresch' (Christ has risen) business resumed below with a bam, boom, and a crash."

About this time the Pleyel company—which had recorded Stravinsky's work on rolls for its player pianos—moved to new quarters in the Faubourg St.-Honoré, where the composer was given a studio. It was here that a serious young violinist, Samuel Dushkin, approached Stravinsky with the idea of writing a work for the violin.

"I hesitated at first," the composer wrote, "because I am not a violinist and I was afraid that my slight knowledge of that instrument would not be sufficient to enable me to solve the many problems which would necessarily arise in the course of a major work specifically composed for it."

After some deliberation Stravinsky agreed to begin the new project, and a meeting was arranged with Dushkin. The young violinist, who had heard that Stravinsky could be difficult and curt with someone he did not like, nervously prepared for their first session.

Agreeably surprised, Dushkin found that

here, among friends, his personal charm was evident at once. It was not long before I realized that he was not only capable of giving tenderness and affection but seemed to be in great need of them himself. In fact, I sensed very soon something tense and anguished about him which made me want to comfort and reassure *him*. The Stravinsky I had heard about and imagined and the Igor Fedorovich I met seemed two different people.

The auspicious beginning ripened into a friendship that was not threatened by the inevitable disagreements which arise when two artists work together. Dushkin's main function was "to advise Stravinsky how his ideas could best be adapted to the exigencies of the violin as a concert display instrument."

As work on the concerto progressed Stravinsky would show Dushkin what he had written and ask for the violinist's comments. When a mutual friend asked Stravinsky if the two were getting along together he answered, "When I show Sam a new passage, he is deeply moved, very excited—then a few days later he asks me to make changes."

Occasionally Dushkin would arrange certain passages and ask for Stravinsky's comments. Often the composer would like them and agree to use them; at other times he refused. At one point Dushkin was delighted with his arrangement and insistently maintained that he wanted the composer to keep it. Stravinsky, who would not be convinced, commented, "You remind me of a salesman at the Galeries Lafayette [a Parisian department store]. You say 'isn't this brilliant, isn't this exquisite, look at the beautiful colors, everybody's wearing it.' I say, 'Yes, it is brilliant, it is beautiful, everyone is wearing it—I don't want it.' "

It was during this collaboration that Dushkin glimpsed Stravinsky's religious attitudes. The violinist had been amazed at how slowly the work of composition progressed. Often he would find Stravinsky at the piano "intensely concentrated, grunting, and struggling to find the notes and chords [he seemed] to be hearing."

When the work was going even more slowly than usual, Stravinsky would sometimes talk of the need for faith. Looking at Dushkin, he would say, "You must have faith. When I was younger, and ideas didn't come, I felt desperate and thought everything was finished. But now I have faith, and I know ideas will come. The waiting in anguish is the price one must pay."

Later, when they had stopped working briefly and were walking in the garden, Stravinsky added, "First ideas are very important; they come from God. And if after working and working and working I return to these ideas, then I know they are good."

Stravinsky's *Violin Concerto* was first performed in

Berlin at the Philharmonic Concert Hall by the Berliner Rundfunk Orchestra. It received a divided press, including a good many outraged and vicious reviews. After they were all in, Dushkin found Stravinsky extremely disturbed.

"Why are you so upset?" he asked the composer. "Hasn't it always been so? Even Voltaire so long ago said, 'The critic is to the artist what the fly is to a race horse. It stings him but doesn't stop him.'"

Stravinsky enjoyed hearing that, but although it calmed him he remained visibly angry. Remembering Stravinsky's interest in religion, Dushkin added, "No one can please everyone. Even God doesn't please everyone."

Stravinsky jumped to his feet and shouted, "*Especially* God!"

It was not long after this that Stravinsky had an opportunity to get back at the critics. Having been asked, with other artists of international prominence, to contribute a few words about Picasso on the occasion of the great 1932 exhibitions of his work in Paris and Zurich, Stravinsky wrote:

If I admire something I admire it unreservedly; and that is certainly the case with Picasso. I admire him as much for what he is doing and has done as for what he will do in the future. I do not criticize him. Criticism is the job of critics; and one knows only too well what that involves. It's no secret that criticism leads to confusion, the substitution of habit for enthusiasm, and the retardation of the appreciation of contemporary artists. Criticism is a profession for persons of ill-will. . . .

Another favorite target for Stravinsky's sharpest criticism was the conductor. His reputation gave rise to many periods of anxiety for young conductors about to conduct his works. A good example was Eugene Goossens, who came to the composer's small studio over the Salle Pleyel a week before he was to conduct the *Piano Concerto.*

Since Goossens had never conducted the work there was much discussion of "tempi," phrasing, and other problems. Stravinsky answered all Goossens' questions but the conductor still seemed insecure in his knowledge of the dynamics of certain passages. He rephrased the questions. Stravinsky listened patiently, then jumped to his feet, good-humoredly thumped the keyboard, and "with an expression of tolerant exasperation" exclaimed, "But my dear fellow, play just what's written and stop worrying!"

Later Goossens wrote:

The responsibility resting on the shoulders of the conductor during the performance of Stravinsky's music is a heavy one. On the one hand, he must avoid the devil of inaccuracy, and on the other, the deep-sea of so-called "interpretation." His sense of musical values must be unerring, and his technical equipment vast! Above all, he must be a wholehearted champion of this music: no mental reservations are possible concerning it.

The year 1930 marked the appearance of one of Stravinsky's most important works. The *Symphony of Psalms,* commissioned by the Boston Symphony Orchestra and now considered one of his masterpieces, revealed depths of feeling often felt to be lacking in Stravinsky's music.

The composer had no desire to imitate the conventional type of nineteenth-century symphony. He had avoided this when composing an earlier work, the *Symphonies of Wind Instruments,* by incorporating several episodes within a single movement. Now, tackling the same problem again, Stravinsky decided that his new work should feature extensive contrapuntal development and that this could best be attained by the use of a chorus that would have equal footing with the orchestra. For his text he chose the whole of Psalm 150 and extracts from Psalms 39 and 40.

The *Symphony of Psalms* is unified by thematic patterns that run through the entire work, including the great double fugue in the second movement. Stravinsky makes use of only the bass registers of the strings; the woodwinds and brasses, which predominate, are responsible for the peculiar timbre of the piece. Its almost unbearable tension is finally resolved in the last movement with a haunting and unforgettable serenity unique in Stravinsky's work.

The *Symphony of Psalms* has brought forth words not often used to describe this composer's work—such as "nobility" and "grandeur." Austere, inward-looking, and reflective, this symphony was acknowledged by informed musicians to be a work of ripe maturity, an undisputed masterpiece.

Meanwhile, as the depression worsened and the franc continued to fall in value, Stravinsky's financial condition improved. Unlike other prominent contemporary composers, such as Prokofiev or Béla Bartók, Stravinsky could live reasonably well from his earnings as a composer and performer. During these years he was constantly traveling throughout Europe, occasionally with Samuel Dushkin and more often with his second eldest son Soulima, who had become an accomplished pianist. And the commissions continued to come in. In 1927 the famous dancer Ida Rubinstein asked him to write a work especially for her ballet, which was subsequently entitled *Perséphone.*

In 1934 Igor Stravinsky became a French citizen—a move that insured the prospect of a considerably larger income. French citizenship cleared up the position of his author's rights and extended them retroactively for three years, so that all his compositions from 1931 on were protected in the United States as well as in France. Everything he had composed prior to that date remained unprotected there, as well as in the U.S.S.R., because both of these countries had failed to sign the Berne copyright agreement.

Although the times of financial crisis seemed to have passed, other worries quickly took their place. In 1934 Stravinsky's hypochondria gained the upper hand. After his eldest son Theodore underwent an emergency appendectomy, the composer himself decided to have the same operation; later he forced similar operations on his other children and even on some of his friends.

This was only the beginning of far more severe physical problems for the Stravinsky family. In 1938 his eldest daughter, Ludmila, age thirty, died of tuberculosis. The following year Catherine died from the same disease; just a few months later Stravinsky's mother died at eighty-five.

Shaken by the long periods of tension and worry that preceded these deaths, Stravinsky was haunted by a sense of still greater changes to come. But such a heightened anxiety about oneself, about Europe, about the world, was almost inevitable during the last years of this decade, which was pervaded by an atmosphere of impending disaster.

At the World's Fair held in Paris in 1937 it did not require any unusual intelligence to see that the extraordinary number of German "tourists" wandering through the exhibits, the city, and the countryside were not interested in French culture and the beauty of the land. With their cameras, maps, and charts they could methodically familiarize themselves with the terrain of the land they were to invade not many years hence. This was also a propitious time to approach possible supporters and organize a network of spies.

Meanwhile the savage civil war in Spain continued; the fall of Madrid signaled a series of organized massacres in Spain that were as cruel and barbarous as any in history. Refugees from central Europe—having seen much recent suffering in their own homelands—were appalled at the sights of famine and ruin they saw as they traveled through Spain toward a temporary haven in Portugal.

Farther east Mussolini continued to bomb and destroy Albania as the first step in his planned invasion of Yugoslavia, which in turn would lead to the old

Italian dream of dominating the eastern shores of the Adriatic. Throughout Europe men feared the spread of these smaller wars, while not far from Stravinsky's studio on the Boulevard St.-Honoré—for the reasonable price of about eighty francs—you could buy a gas mask.

In a radio interview with Serge Moreux, which was broadcast on December 24, 1938, Stravinsky said, "It is hardly astonishing that the critics have lost their sense of direction, for the crisis is certainly more widespread than is at present realized. The state of mankind is deeply affected; knowledge of values and feeling for relationships are submerged. This is extremely serious, for it leads us to transgress the fundamental laws of human equilibrium."

The French were showing less interest in Stravinsky's music; after the great early years with the Russian Ballet the nation had never really been enthusiastic about his work. In the five years between 1935 and 1939 he visited England only twice. And for several years now Nazi Germany had condemned Stravinsky as a purveyor of decadence and forbidden his music to be performed.

In 1938 an exhibition of *Entartete Musik* (Degenerate Music) staged in a Dusseldorf hall attacked not only Stravinsky but Schoenberg, Alban Berg, Paul Hindemith, and Kurt Weill. A recording of Schoenberg's *Pierrot Lunaire* was played and various documents and photographs of the composers were displayed in a highly unflattering manner.

In 1938 Stravinsky was offered the distinguished

Charles Eliot Norton chair of poetry at Harvard, and by late 1939 he had finished the draft of his lectures. These had kept his mind occupied during this year of many crises—the most difficult being the death of his wife, at the age of fifty-seven, on March 2. He was eager to leave Europe, and friends could see that he was "perplexed and jittery . . . he could neither eat nor sleep, he could not work . . . he got angry, nervous, and irritable. All he wanted was to get as quickly as possible out of Paris, out of Europe, and into America, where life was still orderly."

In September 1939—shortly after the outbreak of the war—he embarked on the *Manhattan* for New York. Like many others who saw the United States only as a refuge in time of trouble, Stravinsky did not realize that it was to become his permanent home.

16

EXILES AGAIN

New York in 1939 was filled with refugees from Europe; among them were many of the continent's greatest musicians. Staying in the city as briefly as possible, Stravinsky soon left for Cambridge, Massachusetts, where he lived for just over two months.

Stravinsky's lectures at Harvard attracted large audiences. For students whose knowledge of French was inadequate a concise synopsis of each lecture was prepared in English. The titles of the six lectures, later published as *The Poetics of Music*, were: 1. "Getting Acquainted"; 2. "The Phenomenon of Music"; 3. "The Composition of Music"; 4. "Musical Typology"; 5. "The Avatars of Russian Music"; 6. "The Performance of Music and Epilogue."

Stravinsky also gave a series of talks about music to a small group of advanced students in composition. Outspoken as usual, he quickly indicated errors in counterpoint or style and, when merited, praised original invention and imagination. There was never any formalized instruction during these talks, for Stravinsky —who was never interested in teaching—much preferred an atmosphere of informal criticism. Often, when the discussion was focused on one of his own works, he would play at the piano, stopping from time to time to analyze and explain the composition.

"My instinct," Stravinsky wrote, "is to recompose, and not only students' works, but old masters as well. When composers show me their music for criticism all I can say is that I would have written it quite differently. Whatever interests me, whatever I love, I wish to make my own (I am probably describing a rare form of kleptomania.)"

In December 1939 he returned to New York to meet Vera de Bosset, an old and dear friend who had just arrived from Europe. Verushka, as he affectionately called her, was to become a very important part of Stravinsky's life, for on March 9, 1940, they were married.

Vera Stravinsky, whose life had been as colorful and dramatic as her new husband's, was born in St. Petersburg of French and Swedish ancestry. She was a well-known actress in her youth both on the stage and in films, but this career came to an abrupt end when she fled the revolution with her husband, the painter Sergei Sudekine, in May 1917. After many difficulties the couple finally reached France in May 1920. Several months later Vera Sudekine was introduced to Igor Stravinsky by Diaghilev, thus beginning their long friendship.

Most European refugees limited their choice of American residence to only two cities. One was New

York with its already strong international character and extraordinary cultural life. The other, three thousand miles to the west, was by contrast a quiet town. As one wag commented, it was not a city at all but "seven suburbs in search of a city." Yet it was that very quiet, that atmosphere of remoteness from the disastrous war in Europe, which made Los Angeles so attractive to a large number of European artists and intellectuals.

Los Angeles also had the benefit of an unusually mild climate, which greatly appealed to people who knew only too well the rigors of the European winter. In the open-air markets of Los Angeles and Hollywood there was an abundance of fresh vegetables and fruits throughout the winter; roses and many other flowers hardly ever stopped blooming.

After first considering several other areas of the city Vera and Igor Stravinsky decided on a house high in the Hollywood hills. The tiny house contained only one bedroom but it had a marvelous garden, a terrace, and excellent views of Los Angeles and Beverly Hills.

Although many houses were already being built in the hills north of Sunset Strip, an amazing wildlife still flourished on the edge of the encroaching civilization. Occasionally rattlesnakes were killed by horrified parents who found the snakes sunning themselves on their children's play equipment, and one summer night an opossum charged through an open door and into Igor's study. On another hot night—during one of the long summer droughts that bring the animals toward the houses in a desperate search for water—a small wildcat sprang onto the roof from behind the house.

It was a gay house, not only because of Vera's trained artist's eye but also because of Igor's wide-ranging interests as a collector. Vera described it as "bright and cozy, with light-colored upholstery, pillows, rugs, and a plentiful array of flowers." There was simple American furniture; there were rubber plants in the dining room; and almost every available space was crammed with the Stravinskys' large collection of books and works of art.

The library of ten thousand books could not be contained in the small room set aside for it but spread out into all the other rooms. It was carefully classified by author, subject, and language; art books formed the largest category, with books on poetry taking second place. There was also a large collection of Shakespeare and a number of old Baedekers. Vera said that "Igor is a steady reader, and though he is inclined to pursue an author or subject to a rut, his interests are varied and unpredictable."

Each room housed a part of the art collection, which ranged from posters advertising performances of *Oedipus* and *Perséphone* at the Warsaw Opera to original paintings by Picasso, Klee, Chagall, and many others. The collection was as eclectic as one would expect Stravinsky's to be and included pre-Columbian statues, early American antiques, Igor's family silverware with his mother's crown-shaped coat of arms, and Inca and Copt textiles.

Soon the Stravinskys had a wide circle of friends, including Eugene Berman, the painter; Aldous Huxley, the English writer; and Franz Werfel, the Austrian dramatist and novelist who had written *The Song of Bernadette*. Werfel recalled of Stravinsky:

Frequently I talked with him until late in the night; and our discussion ranged widely over many varied subjects from the latest political scandal to the Epistles of St. Paul, by way of Bach's music, the style of Gide, the relationship between Spinoza and Bergson, Spanish mysticism as revealed in Spanish art, and so on.

The great German writer Thomas Mann claimed that "Hollywood during the war was a more intellectually stimulating and cosmopolitan city than Paris or Munich had ever been." Vera commented, "The ferment of composers, writers, scientists, artists, actors, and philosophers did exist and we often attended the lectures, exhibitions, concerts, performances, and social gatherings of these people ourselves."

When guests came from out of town they were warmly received by the Stravinskys, but because the small house did not contain a guest room they were forced to sleep on a couch in an alcove off the living room.

The studio was the room farthest from the kitchen because Stravinsky could not tolerate any odor while composing and claimed that strong, pungent odors actually interfered with his sense of hearing.

Nicolas Nabokov described Stravinsky's studio as "an extraordinary room, perhaps the best planned and organized work-room I have seen in my life." It was spacious enough to accommodate two pianos—one an upright, the other a grand—and two desks. One was a small elegant writing desk used mainly for correspondence, the other a draftsman's table where Stravinsky worked.

Vera described this desk as "a kind of surgeon's operation table." Neatly arranged on it were a number of colored pencils, erasers, electric pencil-sharpeners, stopwatches, electric metronomes, and the patented styluses Stravinsky invented to print his staves.

Stravinsky was fond of having tea in the late afternoon. Generally he read for a little while before his daily nap. Other diversions were playing solitaire, listening to records, or strolling in the patio and chatting with the gardener Vassili Varzhinsky.

Unlike many people who came to the United States for a safe haven during the war and quickly returned to Europe as soon as it was over, Igor Stravinsky found that he liked the United States so much he wanted to remain. He became a citizen and developed a deep attachment for this country. Stravinsky never permitted criticism of America in his presence; when it came up he interrupted or changed the conversation. Sometimes, without further explanation, he would remark simply but with feeling, "America is good for me."

17

LIFE IN HOLLYWOOD

One characteristic people who knew Igor Stravinsky usually commented on was his ability to immerse himself totally in the present moment. He had little concern for what was past and never expressed regrets, remorse, or nostalgia. It was always the present, the living moment of here and now that absorbed him; from it he sought to extract as much joy and beauty as possible. Perhaps it is his awareness of the poetry and beauty inherent in the living moment that is celebrated in the unique Stravinsky rhythms.

Because of this attitude he was able to adapt himself easily to the many changes in his life, the many removals, the experience of many foreign cultures and traditions.

Related to Stravinsky's concern for the present was his ability to turn whatever came his way to his own good account. Arthur Honegger, the French composer, once complained to him about the problems involved with a new commission he had just received. He was wondering how he would manipulate the balance between one hundred choristers and seventeen instrumentalists—these particular numbers having been insisted upon by those who awarded him the commission. "How can I possibly manage such a curious disproportion?" he asked.

"It's very simple," Stravinsky answered. "Act as if it were you yourself who had chosen this particular combination and compose for your hundred singers and seventeen instrumentalists accordingly."

Honegger said that although Stravinsky's advice might at first appear to be obvious it taught him an important lesson. He realized that one should see a commission not as something imposed from without but as a "personal point of departure responding to inner necessity."

Many years later, when Stravinsky was asked to comment on the idea of patronage and it was pointed out to him that he had always worked on commission, the composer phrased his thinking differently. "The trick, of course, is to choose one's commission, to compose what one wants to compose and get it commissioned afterwards."

It was Stravinsky's adaptability, his endless curiosity and interest in people that drew visitors to the small house in the Hollywood hills. Two who became "dear and intimate friends—loved ones in fact"—were the English writers Christopher Isherwood and Aldous Huxley.

Stravinsky had first heard Isherwood's name when the French writer André Maurois recommended that he read his famous book on Germany in the 1920's, *The Berlin Stories*. Later, when Stravinsky met Isherwood in Hollywood, he was "astonished by how exactly the 'Chris' of the stories he was. The question of 1. 'my art' and 2. 'my life' did not exist for him. His books were himself, and he slipped in and out of them without so much as zipping a zipper."

Stravinsky's fondness for Christopher Isherwood developed the evening that Isherwood first visited at his house. Someone put on a recording of some works by the composer and Isherwood promptly fell asleep. "My affection for him began with that incident," Stravinsky wrote. "I soon discovered that conversation with him may appear to be relaxed, but is actually full of undertow . . . Christopher is a passionately loyal friend, and I feel very close to him."

Aldous Huxley was described by Stravinsky as "the most aristocratic man I have ever known, and I do not mean in the sense of birth. . . . Aldous is an aristocrat of behavior. He is gentle, humble, courageous, intellectually charitable. Of the learned people I know, he is the most delectable conversationalist, and of that breed he is one of the few who are always droll."

Stravinsky and Huxley liked to lunch at the Farmers' Market, where one could choose from a wide variety of foreign foods and eat in the warm, gentle air of the California outdoors. Afterward they went to concerts, plays, and film previews, explored Southern California museums, zoological gardens, and architectural oddities. "I remember him," Stravinsky wrote, "in the San Diego Zoo referring to each caged creature by its Latin name while revealing fascinating facts about its sexual habits and I.Q. I remember him peering at a huge Los

Angeles bank in construction next to a tiny church and murmuring something about 'God and Mammon in the usual proportion . . . .' "

Stravinsky is himself known for his quick, acerbic responses and wit. One day Samuel Dushkin found him somewhat worried about his physical condition and asked what was the matter. Stravinsky answered, "Oh, my intestines, my intestines!"

"Do they hurt?" Dushkin inquired.

"No, they don't hurt," Stravinsky answered, "but they keep saying, 'We are here, we are here'!"

Once Stravinsky gave a good deal of time to an attractive young woman he seemed to find amusing. "I feel so much when I hear *Firebird* and *Pétrouchka*," she said. "Why can't I feel anything in your later works?"

"My dear," Stravinsky replied, "for that you'll have to consult your doctor."

Another time he wisely commented to someone who was hurrying, "Why do you hurry? *I have no time to hurry.*"

Nicolas Nabokov wrote that when Stravinsky turned his wit toward stupid people, musicians, or scores he did not like it was "a scathing, pitiless kind of humor which knows no bounds."

In a filing cabinet under his piano, in a separate folder, Stravinsky kept choice pictures of conductors in highly contorted poses. Most of these pictures were taken from publicity releases or newspapers. It was for such conductors that the composer reserved his sharpest and most picturesque remarks. He said that an overly emotional, too exuberant conductor reminded him of a "danse du ventre vu par derrière" (an Oriental belly dance seen from behind). His wildly gesticulating arms reminded Stravinsky of a pair of egg beaters.

"Look at him!" the composer would say with exasperation as he pointed to the pictures in the folder. "Look at the dandy! Look at his idiotic expression, his frothy gestures. Is all this nonsense necessary to conduct an orchestra?"

In Hollywood—as in Paris—Stravinsky attended the Russian Orthodox church, a tiny white building with blue onion domes, about twenty-five minutes from the Stravinsky house.

He was particularly fond of the Russian Easter service, which is celebrated at night. Just before midnight those in the open-air congregation (the church is too small to hold everyone) light tapers. Exactly at twelve the church doors are flung open, and the clergy and the small congregation who have managed to get inside now join with those outside.

The deacon leads the procession, swinging the censer and spreading incense that pervades the group. A few paces behind him the bishop—in scarlet, white, and gold samite—pauses on the top step and sings "Christos Voskresch" (Christ is Risen). The congregation responds "Vieestinoo Voskresch" (He is indeed). After the bishop comes a priest carrying a tall cross, followed by a group of acolytes carrying Russian icons, *haroogvee* (holy banners or icons made of cloth), and the globe and scepter of Christ the King.

All the clerics have the traditional long beards of the

Russian Orthodox clergy. They parade around the church three times, calling "Christos Voskresch" each time and each time receiving the response "Vieestinoo Voskresch."

When the service is concluded there is much kissing —Russian style, three times for each person. And there is no escape, for Easter kisses are not refusable.

Afterward, although they did not observe the Lenten Fast, the Stravinskys celebrated with the traditional foods such as *kooleetch*, the Easter bread, and an Easter cake called *paska*, a delicious dish made of sugar, milk, cheese, eggs, raisins, and tutti-frutti.

It was inevitable that Stravinsky, living in Hollywood, would be offered films to score. Negotiations were begun in several instances but they never came to fruition. When asked what he thought of music in films the composer answered, "It shouldn't be used, except where logically required by context, which could mean not only in views of concerts but in the imagination of a musically minded character. There can be no real relationship between what one sees and what one hears, but only habit relationships, all of them bad."

Other ventures in the entertainment world were more attractive to Stravinsky and proved successful. In 1942 he was asked by The Ringling Bros. Barnum & Bailey Circus to write a polka especially for a troupe of young elephants to dance in a ballet. (The elephants were to wear differently colored ballet tutus.) Stravinsky accepted this offer with delight, and the resulting "Circus Polka" became extremely successful.

In 1944 the Broadway producer Billy Rose offered

Stravinsky $5,000 to write a fifteen-minute ballet suite for a new show called *The Seven Lively Arts*. Stravinsky accepted the commission, wrote the music, and waited to hear how the production fared on Broadway. After the first night of the preview he received the following telegram from Billy Rose: YOUR MUSIC GREAT SUCCESS STOP COULD BE SENSATION IF YOU WOULD AUTHORIZE ROBERT RUSSELL BENNETT RETOUCH ORCHESTRATION STOP BENNETT ORCHESTRATES EVEN THE WORKS OF COLE PORTER.

Igor Stravinsky immediately wired back: SATISFIED WITH GREAT SUCCESS.

Another commission developed out of Stravinsky's interest in the artistry of Woody Herman. A leader of one of the country's best jazz bands, Herman was an informed and talented musician. *The Ebony Concerto,* written especially for him, dates from 1945.

In order to write this work Stravinsky had to study such instruments as the guitar and the saxophone, and he had to become acquainted with the techniques of the jazz band—all music-making components of which he had no experience. Since Woody Herman is a virtuoso of the clarinet, this instrument was given a prominent part in the concerto. Ingenious and delightful, this piece was still another example of the way Stravinsky could make the fullest use of the musical tradition and still indelibly stamp it with his own personality.

Even in the healthy California climate, Stravinsky's concern for his physical well-being remained as obsessive as ever. His bathroom in the new house was filled with a wide and unusual variety of medicines.

There were long rows of blue-white porcelain apothecary jars, trays of syringes, and a varied selection of hot-water bottles. Every medicine was carefully labeled in Russian by Stravinsky himself.

Vera told a friend that the "powders, the unguents and ointments, the drops, the herbs and other material medicines are so mixed up with the sacred medals that I fear he will swallow a Saint Christopher some night instead of a sleeping pill."

The extraordinary thing about Stravinsky's concern with himself and his physical well-being is that it never interfered with his extremely sensitive perception of the world without. A friend, having found him somewhat disturbed one morning, asked what was the matter.

"I haven't had my sleep," the composer explained. "I was awakened at dawn this morning by a little bird singing on my window sill. For the first five minutes I was fascinated. But the bird went on singing. After *ten* minutes I wanted to kill that bird. But the bird went on singing. And do you know, after fifteen minutes, I was again fascinated."

18

THE RAKE'S PROGRESS

For many years Stravinsky had wanted to write an opera in English but a suitable subject had eluded him. Then, one day while at an exhibition of English paintings and engravings at the Art Institute in Chicago, it occurred to him that Hogarth's famous series *The Rake's Progress* provided an excellent basis for a "series of operatic scenes."

William Hogarth was one of many eighteenth-century painters to focus on the daily life of his own times rather than the religious themes that had occupied most artists in previous centuries. A series of engravings based on Hogarth's oil paintings became extremely popular during the artist's lifetime and has since become one of the best sources of reference material for the society and morals of the eighteenth century.

Shortly after his return to Hollywood Stravinsky discussed his plan with Aldous Huxley, who immediately suggested the poet W. H. Auden as the librettist. Auden, who was delighted with the idea, soon left his home in New York for Hollywood, where he joined the Stravinskys as a house guest and became, in the process, still another famous artist whose feet stuck out over the edges of the couch.

From the beginning Stravinsky was sure that he wanted to write an opera in what he called the "Italian-Mozartian" style; he told a friend he intended to "lace each aria into a tight corset." While Auden was staying with him in the autumn of 1947 they attended a two-piano performance of *Cosi fan Tutte,* which was the only music Stravinsky would listen to while composing *The Rake's Progress.*

W. H. Auden gave Stravinsky the final version of the libretto in March 1948 and at the same time introduced him to a young man—then only twenty-four—who was to become an important part of his future life.

Igor Stravinsky and Robert Craft felt rapport with each other from their first meeting, and soon afterward the composer invited the young man to join his household in Hollywood as a kind of secretary-assistant.

One of his first jobs was to pronounce and repeat the lines of the libretto for *The Rake's Progress* so that Stravinsky might learn the sounds and rhythms of the words and fit them to music. For example, as Craft wrote, "there were not enough notes to cover the final syllables of 'questioning,' 'initiated,' and 'gentlemen.'" When this was pointed out to him Stravinsky easily made the necessary changes.

Although Stravinsky could easily have had the premiere of his opera in any of the world's great opera houses, he had no difficulty in deciding on Venice's Teatro La Fenice. It has a more intimate quality than most of the other important houses, and the general scale of *The Rake's Progress,* both vocally and instrumentally, is on the small side.

In Italy Igor Stravinsky was welcomed with the enthusiasm usually reserved for film stars or statesmen. At the Hotel Duomo in Milan the street was blocked off, its entrance protected by ropes.

After some preliminary work in Milan, Stravinsky, his party, the cast, chorus, and orchestra traveled in three reserved railway cars to Venice. Shortly afterward Robert Craft saw Stravinsky's piano "trussed in canvas and hawsers . . . pulleyed from the canal to his second-floor room like a horse up the side of a ship."

After morning rehearsals Stravinsky, often accompanied by Robert Craft, Vera, and Auden, renewed his acquaintance with the endless beauties and wonders of this incomparable city. In midsummer the main event of the season—the Venetian Regatta—drew crowds to the city, giving it an even more festive air. By midafternoon of the great day almost every boat in Venice was gathered in the Grand Canal—sailboats, gondolas, motorboats, and others—all bearing the standard of Venice's patron, St. Mark.

By night the city was magical with the familiar Venetian sounds of water lapping on stone, oars plashing in the canals, the iron shutters of shop fronts clanging down, and the cries of the gondoliers, the soft singing of women from the darkened houses.

One day Robert Craft and Auden crossed the Laguna Morta (Lagoon of Death) to the island of Torcello, where they placed a wreath on Diaghilev's grave in the famous cemetery of San Michele—unaccompanied by Stravinsky, who superstitiously refused to go near the island.

On September 11, the day of the premiere, the weather was damp and Auden, who was impatient with the stage director, threatened to change the line "a scene like this is better than a sale" to "a scene like this is slower than a snail." Nevertheless, when the curtain finally went up, in spite of several wrong entrances and dozens of mistakes, the performance was a memorable one for everyone concerned.

The first-night audience at Teatro La Fenice was elegant as only an Italian audience can be. The men were all in evening dress; the women extraordinarily beautiful in a dazzling array of furs, gowns, and gleaming jewels.

Robert Craft wrote that

. . . when the lights were dimmed and Stravinsky entered the pit, the applause that greeted him stratified into three areas: from the entire house came a general applause that paid tribute to his great stature (what he called his "credientials"); from the expensive seats, an applause of welcome for a major social event; from the galleries, the applause of expectancy in the promise of a master at the height of his powers presenting his largest work.

As usual, Stravinsky conducted with a dignity, an understanding, and an intensity that no other conductor could bring to his music. By the end of the second act there was an excitement and enthusiasm appropriate to the first performance of a great opera.

The Rake's Progress does not break new ground, as did so many of Stravinsky's great works. In a general statement written for the first American production in 1953, the composer stated that *The Rake's Progress* is "emphatically, an opera, an opera of arias and recitatives, choruses and ensembles. Its musical structure, the conception of these forms, even to the relations of tonalities, is in the line of the classical tradition."

Auden's libretto—actually a work of collaboration with his friend Chester Kallman—did not literally follow the Hogarth story. The action, which covers a full year, begins when Tom Rakewell (tenor), a handsome young Englishman, is informed by a messenger called Nick Shadow (baritone) that an unknown uncle has just died and that Tom is his heir.

After saying goodbye to his sweetheart, Ann Trulove (soprano), Tom engages Shadow as his servant for a year and leaves for London, where he plans to claim his estate. Tom's new wealth permits him a life of pleasure but after a while he becomes bored. When Tom becomes increasingly tired of his sensuous, indulgent life, Nick Shadow—the personification of evil—urges him to commit a gratuitous act, a wanton act of freedom that accomplishes nothing other than the assertion of the will. (Perhaps one of the most famous of such acts is Raskolnikov's murder of the old woman in Dostoevski's *Crime and Punishment*.)

Following this counsel Tom marries Baba the Turk (mezzo-soprano), who has become one of the main attractions of St. Giles Fair due to her luxurious beard. The marriage fails as Tom nears bankruptcy. His final castastrophe comes when Nick Shadow's year of service is concluded and he leads Tom at midnight to a churchyard where there is a newly dug grave. When they arrive he reveals himself as the devil and claims Tom's soul as his wages.

The devil offers Tom a choice of ways in which he can take his own life but finally yields to the Rake's plea that his fate be decided by a game of cards. Amazingly, Tom wins, but the devil, having lost, still manages to put a curse of insanity on him. The opera ends in Bedlam (an English insane asylum), where the Rake, now a victim of delusions, is found by his old sweetheart, Ann Trulove. He begs forgiveness and dies.

The major characters return to the stage for the Epilogue, without their wigs. Underscoring the moral of the fable, they sing:

> So let us sing as one.
> At all times in all lands
> Beneath the moon and sun,
> This proverb has proved true,
> Since Eve went out with Adam:
> For idle hands
> And hearts and minds
> The devil finds
> A work to do,
> A work, dear Sir, fair Madam,
> For you—and you!

Once again in *The Rake's Progress* we hear the rhythmic energy of Stravinsky's earlier works. Unlike many operas, it has no sections in which the music becomes a kind of supporting filler. After the premiere and subsequent performances reviews throughout the world were lavish with praise.

Joseph Kennan in *The Hudson Review* wrote:

The Rake . . . seems to me the most genuine and the most delightful work of the theatre in years, to say nothing of its being an operatic masterpiece on almost any terms. . . . I myself think that the librettist's part in the opera has been only slightly less brilliant than Stravinsky's and that indeed the work offers a unique delight to the combined musical and poetic sensibilities.

After the premiere of *The Rake's Progress*, when the final curtain rang down, Stravinsky was given an ovation. Teatro La Fenice resounded with calls of praise as the audience rose to its feet and called, "Bravo! Bravo!" The theater was not cleared until 1:00 A.M. and Stravinsky and his party did not get to bed until after 6:00.

From the theater they went to a famous Venetian restaurant called The Taverina, where they indulged in what Robert Craft called "a tune detection game of citing resemblances to other operas." Vera said she thought the mourning chorus began like the "Volga Boatmen's Song." Auden noted that the beginning of Act II, especially the woodwind trill, reminded him of the dance apprentices in *Die Meistersinger;* the Terzetto he found "Tchaikovskyan"; and he maintained that the Epilogue was modeled on *Don Giovanni.*

Although the composer refused to acknowledge any of these "borrowings," he did admit with a smile that "some of *The Rake* is close to Broadway." For any other composer it would have been an unthinkable admission. For Stravinsky, who was able to magically transmute whatever he wished into something uniquely his own, it was simply an acknowledgment of another source that had been called on to feed his remarkable powers of invention.

Once again a turning point had been reached in Stravinsky's long life. *The Rake's Progress* seemed to be the culmination of his interest in the past; henceforward he would turn in another direction—one that would take him into a world of music where many listeners would find it difficult to follow.

19

SERIAL PERIOD AND RETURN TO RUSSIA

Just a short drive from Igor Stravinsky's home in the Hollywood hills lived the other reigning master of twentieth-century music, Arnold Schoenberg. "Musicians came from all over the world to visit them," Robert Craft wrote, " . . . not mentioning to one composer their meeting with the other one." For eleven years the two composers lived close to each other; for eleven years they did not meet. "Whether it was too late for a musical exchange is no matter," Craft continued; " . . . the important thing is that both composers would have been pleased. We know that Schoenberg had wanted to defend Stravinsky against a Schoenberg disciple; we knew then that Stravinsky was genuinely distressed by the monstrous universal neglect of Schoenberg."

The world had ignored Schoenberg for a long time, but then so had a good many musicians as well. Stravinsky had written, after first hearing *Pierrot Lunaire*, that he did not feel the slightest enthusiasm about this piece. However, with the passage of time his evaluation of Schoenberg's music underwent a radical change.

Writing in 1962, he affirmed in an outburst of admiration for the great innovator that "*Pierrot* is not only the mind but also the solar plexus of early twentieth-century music." He candidly admitted that "it was beyond me as it was beyond all of us at the time." Furthermore, Stravinsky now saw that Schoenberg's *Five Pieces for Orchestra, Erwartung,* and *Die Glückliche Hand* were seminal works in the development of modern music.

Both composers had met from time to time when they lived in Europe. Stravinsky recalled that the Austrian composer was even shorter than himself, with a wreath of black hair around the cranium like a Japanese actor's mask. Schoenberg had large ears and a soft, deep voice; the German he spoke was in a mellow Viennese accent. His eyes were protuberant and "the whole force of the man was in them."

Stravinsky saw Schoenberg for the last time in 1949, when he appeared onstage at a concert and read "a delicately ironic speech acknowledging the honor of the freedom of the city of Vienna just conferred on him, a half-century too late, by the Austrian consul."

The Rake's Progress was the largest work Stravinsky had ever written. It was in a way the summation, the final statement of a major period in his life. Perhaps he now felt that the neoclassical vein had been exhausted and that he must find a new direction for his future work. Also, the recent death of Arnold Schoenberg—just a few weeks before the premiere of *The Rake's Progress*—meant that the three chief exponents of serial music (Arnold Schoenberg, Alban Berg, and Anton Webern) were now dead; perhaps the time had come for serial music to take a new direction with a different master guiding its destiny.

Although in January and February of 1952 Stravinsky was studying Webern's Quartet Op. 22 with great concentration, he apparently was still not ready to give up his earlier views. In May of this year, when an interviewer brought up the question of serial music, Stravinsky replied:

Serialism? Personally I find quite enough to do with seven notes of the scale. Nevertheless the serial composers are the only ones with a discipline that I respect. Whatever else serial music may be, it is certainly pure music. Only, the serialists are prisoners of the figure twelve, while I feel greater freedom with the figure seven.

Nevertheless, Stravinsky continued his study of serial music, with emphasis on the works of Anton Webern rather than those of Schoenberg. The more he studied Webern the greater became his admiration for him; during this period Stravinsky wrote:

The 15th of September, 1945, the day of Anton Webern's death, should be a day of mourning for any receptive musician. We must hail this man not only as a great composer but also as a real hero. Doomed to a total failure in a deaf world of ignorance and indifference, he inexorably kept on cutting out his diamonds, his dazzling diamonds, the mines of which he had such perfect knowledge.

Stravinsky had lost a vast number of admirers when he departed from the folklore of his first period for the neoclassic; now, as he committed himself to serialism, he was about to lose many more.

His old friend Ernest Ansermet had always been opposed to the twelve-tone technique, and when the two met again in 1960 the conversation quickly turned to Stravinsky's latest works using the serial method.

Explaining his objections, Ansermet said, "Suppose you are the producer of a play which has the important line 'Morituri te Salutant' and suppose you cast a separate player for each of these eight syllables. You then reverse the order of the syllables and alter it perhaps in other ways too, ending up with a shout in which all eight syllables are synchronized. Would you understand what this was supposed to mean?"

"No," replied Stravinsky, "I would not necessarily understand it; but it might make an interesting effect."

It was not difficult for Igor Stravinsky to foresee that a new work in the serial method might sell only 3,000 or 4,000 copies (a new recording of *The Firebird* sells 30,000 to 40,000). But the time had come, of course, when money—although still of great importance to Stravinsky—was no longer a consideration when choosing among different commissions or directions in which he wished to go.

Several of Stravinsky's works composed during the 1950's have elements of the serial technique. Of these (*Cantata, Septet,* the *Shakespeare* songs, the *Canticum Sacrum, Agon,* and *In Memoriam Dylan Thomas*) the latter is one of the most interesting as a guide to understanding Stravinsky's approach to twelve-tone music.

In the vocal part of the *Dylan Thomas* piece Stravinsky has strictly applied the serial technique but in this instance the row is five-note, not twelve-note. The resulting experimentation reveals the composer's interest in probing and perhaps developing the twelve-tone technique.

The *Canticum Sacrum* was first performed in St. Mark's Cathedral in Venice, that city so beloved by both Stravinsky and Diaghilev. Like many previous works, it confounded the critics, who found it austere and too derivative of works by leading serial composers, and who gave it a generally cool reception. It was difficult for reviewers as well as for longtime admirers of Stravinsky to find him writing so consistently in the serial technique; as usual, their reservations did not prevent him from giving all his attention to plans for new twelve-tone works.

Threni, written in 1957–58 and commissioned by the Nordeutscher Rundfunk (North German Network) of Hamburg, was Stravinsky's first wholly twelve-tone composition. After its performance it was easier to review the previous pieces that employed the serial technique and that led to this important development.

As always in the past, informed musicians were impressed by the fact that Stravinsky had been able to imprint his own personality so strongly on his material —in this case despite the relatively unyielding restrictions of the serial method. They were delighted by the richness and extent of his serial melody and agreed that the musical textures of these works had a greater intensity than those of his predecessors. As always there was no lack of controversy among the public and the critics.

In 1957 Stravinsky wrote:

Nothing is likely about masterpieces, least of all where there will be any. Nevertheless, a masterpiece is more likely to happen to the composer with the most highly developed language. This language is serial at present and though our contemporary development of it could be tangential to an evolution we do not yet see, for us this doesn't matter. Its resources have enlarged our present language and changed our perspective in it. Developments in language are not easily abandoned and the composer who fails to take account of them may lose the mainstream. Masterpieces aside, it seems to me the new music will be serial.

Almost half a century had passed since Igor Stravinsky had been in Russia; during this long absence his reputation there suffered many vicissitudes.

The period immediately following the 1917 revolution was characterized by experimental, controversial works in all the arts. The Commissar of Public Education, Anatoli Lunacharsky, told Sergei Prokofiev in 1918, "You are a revolutionary in music, we are revolutionaries in life. We ought to work together."

Victor Belayev, an important figure in Russian music circles, said that Stravinsky "must be regarded as one of the most Russian composers who have ever existed." He called *Les Noces* "a work of profound national importance."

During the 1930's, when Joseph Stalin gained power, the cultural scene underwent drastic changes, all of them disastrous from the point of view of experimental artists.

This was the period of Socialist Realism, when Western trends were branded as "Formalism." Dimitri Shostakovich was publicly castigated in 1936 and soon afterward Stravinsky was identified with the corrupt Western bourgeoisie by Arnold Alshavang, who wrote: "Stravinsky is an important . . . artistic ideologist of the imperialist bourgeoisie. With startling receptivity he has captured all the trends, all the changes in the psychology of his class; and together with his class, in these recent years, he is moving swiftly to his doom."

This was the situation that existed until the period after Stalin's death in 1953, often referred to as "The Thaw." A more liberal, relaxed era began in which relationships with foreign artists were established and plans made for a program of cultural exchanges.

When several Russian composers and musicians were attending an international music festival at the University of California in 1961, they brought an official invitation asking Stravinsky to return to Russia and to conduct a concert of his own music on the occasion of his eightieth birthday. Stravinsky had heard of this offer but he remembered the long-standing hostility of the Soviet regime and tried to avoid the delegation; they surprised him in the greenroom of a hall where he had just conducted a concert.

Stravinsky was noncommittal on this occasion and spent the next several months listening to the advice of friends, half of whom urged him to accept while the other half counseled against the trip.

While he was considering his decision, the Russians were making it increasingly clear that works by Stravinsky were no longer taboo within the Soviet Union. In January of 1962 *Pétrouchka* was revived with great success in Moscow and the Moscow Philharmonic gave an excellent performance of the *Symphonies of Wind Instruments.*

Finally Stravinsky decided to return to Russia but felt it necessary to state:

Nostalgia has no part in my proposed visit to Russia. My wish to go there is due primarily to the evidence of a genuine desire or need for me by the younger generation of Russian musicians. No artist's name has been more abused in the Soviet Union than mine, but one cannot achieve the future we must achieve with the Russians by nursing a grudge.

After much preparation the great moment came on September 21, 1962; Igor Stravinsky, wearing dark glasses, bent and leaning on his malacca cane, arrived at Moscow's Shermetievo Airport, and bowed deeply at the head of the landing stairs. Observers were moved by this solemn gesture toward the country of his birth and saw further evidence, as the tour continued, of Stravinsky's deep feeling for Russia, regardless of the many disclaimers.

Rehearsals with the Russian National Orchestra began the following day. The first concert, conducted by the composer and Robert Craft, included *The Rite of Spring, Orpheus,* and the *Ode* Stravinsky had written in memory of Serge Koussevitzky's wife. It was enormously successful, and in response to the overwhelming applause Stravinsky came to the stage where he told the audience, "You see a very happy man."

One of the last events of the visit was a glittering evening reception given by the Soviet Minister of Culture. Many Soviet composers had been invited, including Dimitri Shostakovich and Aram Khachaturian. Each toasted Stravinsky and suggested that he return to Russia permanently. Although he was lauded as a great man, there was still a curious silence about his work. Only Shostakovich toasted his future work.

But Stravinsky himself was deeply moved by the congenial Russian atmosphere—as he was by the entire trip to Russia. When he rose to speak, he said:

. . . the smell of the Russian earth is different, and such things are impossible to forget. . . . A man has one birthplace, one fatherland, one country—he can have but one country—and the place of his birth is the most important factor in his life. I regret that circumstances separated me from my fatherland, that I did not bring my works to birth there and, above all, that I was not there to help the new Soviet Union create its new music. But I did not leave Russia only by my own will, even though I admit I dislike much in my Russia and in Russia generally—but the right to criticize Russia is mine, because Russia is mine and because I love it. I do not give any foreigner that right.

Not long before the Stravinskys left they were summoned to the Kremlin to meet Chairman Nikita Khrushchev, then the dominant figure in the Russian government. Vera told him how beautiful Moscow seemed to them and he replied, "Yes, not long ago I drove around and really looked at it and I was impressed myself, but for eight hundred years it was a pigsty." Khrushchev also repeated the invitation to return permanently to the Soviet Union and promised Stravinsky a *dacha* (country house) in the Crimea, a beautiful area in the southwest of the country.

After they had all returned home Robert Craft wrote in his diary, "I am certain that to be recognized and acclaimed as a Russian in Russia, and to be performed there, has meant more to him than anything else in the years I have known him."

20

BRAVO, STRAVINSKY!

Igor Stravinsky, who had witnessed the rise and fall of so many art movements, cultural revolutions, and upheavals in society, was not surprised by the major changes that had come about in the neighborhood of his Hollywood home during the years of his residence. His house was just a few hundred yards north of Sunset Strip, which was, when the Stravinskys first arrived, one of the most elegant streets in the world. On "The Strip" you could visit some of the finest shops and restaurants in America. By the middle of the 1960's they had all moved, and the neighborhood became a kind of large-scale happening.

Hundreds of long-haired "flower people" lounged on the sidewalks and streets or chatted in such places as "The Body Shop—Kama Sutra is Here." Although Igor Stravinsky was well aware of the atmosphere of protest just minutes from his home the general pattern of his life was little changed since the early 1940's when he had first arrived. But he quickly admitted that the traffic jams, the noise, and the weirdly painted people congregating on the street corners sometimes made life more difficult.

Even in his eighties, Stravinsky did not look his years. There was little gray in his reddish hair, and his eyes and ears had lost none of their sharp sensitivity. Although his face became heavier with the passing of time, it was not marked by the wrinkles characteristic of so many octogenarians.

Once a very fast walker, Stravinsky had to walk very slowly and with a cane. When the distance to be covered was more than a few hundred feet it was necessary to use a wheelchair; the fear of becoming more dependent on this wheelchair was one of the worst anxieties of these years.

People close to Stravinsky were more impressed with the changes in his temperament than those of his body. Although he exhibited some of the usual earmarks of advanced age, such as suspiciousness of remarks he did not understand at once, and an occasional forgetfulness, Vera wrote that the exceptional change was "a new gentleness. Indeed, the word 'gentle' appears so frequently in his vocabulary now, but was so rare in the past, that I accustom myself to it with difficulty."

Consequently there were no longer the great rages and temper tantrums of Stravinsky's youth and middle age, "but only small eruptions that quickly turn to embers." In the past, Vera remembered, "an explosion a week was the uninfractured rule; though what marvelous detonations some of them were, especially when furniture was overturned and crockery smashed. . . ."

Although he appeared to have given way to such rages whenever he liked—presumably releasing emotional tension—Stravinsky also seemed sometimes to require long periods of brooding. On such occasions, Vera said, "Igor could fill a room with his black mood by the simple act of passing through it, like a cuttlefish spreading its black ink."

The composer's extraordinary concern with his health continued unabated and eventually involved even the most casual visitor to the house; for almost any complaint they mentioned he had a remedy at hand. Most of the time he took his own temperature only once a day, but when he became ill he did so much more frequently.

Digestion was also of the utmost importance. Vera wrote that "he will never allow Nature to take its course, at least not without giving it a good nudge. Every meal is dispatched with two tablets of 'concentrated saliva,' a Japanese confection that is said to stimulate digestion."

Another marked Stravinsky characteristic was the composer's feeling for animals; he claimed to feel closer to some of these than to most human beings. He adopted stray kittens and even interrupted work in progress to watch animal programs on television.

When traveling Stravinsky visited zoos before art galleries. During the 1950's, when he spent a part of each summer in Venice, he formed a habit of going to the area of the Scuola di San Fantin, where he fed the large colony of homeless cats that live there.

When the Stravinskys first moved to the Hollywood hills they kept chickens and would have added cows, goats, and a whole barnyard as well but for the zoning laws and the neighbors, who, the composer said, wanted every lawn to look "as tidy as a cemetery or a golf course."

There were times when the Stravinsky house resembled a large birdcage. Often the canaries had the run of the living room, while in the dining room parakeets took turns pecking food directly from Stravinsky's mouth.

Throughout the years Robert Craft, affectionately called "Bobinsky," became an increasingly important figure in Stravinsky's life. He accompanied the composer and his wife on their many trips abroad, organized and conducted concerts of new Stravinsky works, and wrote several books as co-author with the composer. Most of them, taking the form of conversations between Craft and Stravinsky, are a wonderful record of the composer's long life, the extraordinary number of encounters with famous people, reflections on art, life, and of course, music and musicians. Unlike the somewhat staid and pompous earlier autobiography, they are clever, witty, and intensely personal.

The books have been read avidly and have no doubt enlarged Stravinsky's audience and reputation. Because of the dual authorship the question has arisen concerning how much the style can be attributed to Stravinsky and how much to Craft. On this point *New York Times* music critic Harold C. Schoenberg has written: "Surely those bright, tart, rapier-like observations and judgments are Stravinsky's own. And sometimes he uses a club rather than a rapier. . . . Stravinsky cares about nobody's reputation, and he is not concerned where his blows will fall. . . ."

Many honors came to Igor Stravinsky in his later years. In 1954 he was given the Gold Medal of the Royal Philharmonic Society, London; in 1956 he was awarded the Jan Sibelius Gold Medal by the Cultural Foundation of Finland. The following year Stravinsky was elected a Fellow of the American Academy of Arts and Letters, and in 1962 Pope John XXIII conferred on him the honor of Knight Commander of St. Sylvester.

In 1963 he was awarded the Wihuri-Sibelius prize by Wihuri's Foundation for International Prizes. A year later the Mayor of Jerusalem presented him with the golden emblem of Jerusalem on the occasion of the first performance of the sacred ballad for baritone and chamber orchestra, *Abraham and Isaac*. In January 1962 he was the guest of honor at a White House dinner given by President and Mrs. Kennedy.

Although never one to give particular concern to the future of young musicians, Igor Stravinsky in recent years expressed his views on the young composer and the world of contemporary music.

Performance outlets available to him are few . . . and the circuits heavily loaded. The young composer's musical position . . . could be described as a variety of dilemmas . . . his . . . teachers . . . instead of helping him, only bewilder him the more by their own ever more cynical departures on the seasonal bandwagons. Never before have composers been so unprepared by their schooling. The composition techniques still generally taught are as useful as spare parts for machinery last manufactured about seventy-five years ago.

Stravinsky, who never had good things to say for music critics, understood that today it is often difficult for a composer to overcome the impressions made by his first works. "A bad, meaning unfavorable, review may have disastrous consequences for a gifted young composer whose work probably cannot be evaluated on a single hearing in any case."

Stravinsky felt that he was able to have an easy relationship with the young:

I attribute my own rapport with them, a better one than I had with their parents and grandparents at that age . . . to the natural desire to cling to an old man in hopes that he can point the road to the future. What is needed, of course, is simply *any* road that offers enough mileage and a good enough safety record. And my road satisfies these requirements, though the direction in which it extends is not the future but the past.

Even in his eighties Stravinsky took delight in marking, with strong red-ink lines, passages about himself in books and articles that he considered idiotic. However, Vera said that "Igor is fond of bad reviews and they are important to his security. Consider, after all, that he has hardly ever had a good one, and then look at those who have them all the time."

Marcel Proust, to whom Stravinsky had insisted so

long ago that he detested Beethoven, would have been pleased to hear that

. . . at eighty I have found new joy in Beethoven, and the Great Fugue now seems to me—it was not always so—a perfect miracle. How right Beethoven's friends were when they convinced him to detach it from Opus 130, for it must stand by itself, this absolutely contemporary piece of music that will be contemporary forever. . . .

Stravinsky . . . Stravinsky! More than any other, this name dominated the music of the twentieth century. With dramatic suddenness his inventive genius brought forth an amazing number of wonderful works for the theater. First dazzled by the forward thrust of his wide-ranging originality, the world was then astonished to find this destroyer of traditions returning to those very traditions—to rework them into an art unmistakably his own. When he turned toward serial music he was able, as always, to stamp it with his own strong personality.

No composer of the past hundred years has evoked more controversy than Stravinsky. As an extraordinary catalyst, he aroused musicologists, conductors, and critics to a lively and continuing musical dispute. Books, articles, and conversations bristling with pro-and-con Stravinsky sentiments are a large part of the musical history of our time.

Several books could be filled with either condemnations of, or tributes to, Igor Stravinsky. Often critics have found that the dazzling textures and inventiveness obscure what is really an absence of true feeling, of human warmth; others have commented on a seemingly predatory exploitation of musical traditions.

Paul Henry Lang has written that Stravinsky can "at his best achieve dignity and resonance, but seldom real intimacy . . . there is almost a greater interest in impeccable style and manner than the message."

But Stravinsky—like his contemporary, Picasso—rises above such considerations as those of intimacy or message. By themselves his several masterpieces are enough to secure his position as one of the greatest composers of the twentieth century, but it is the total output, the amazing range, the inexhaustible fecundity that give Stravinsky a unique place in the hierarchy of artists.

It appears to be an instinctive part of every human being to be drawn to those unique individuals who have been able to make contact with that great source of cosmic energy, of Being, of what Stravinsky called "a system beyond nature."

Surely some of these men, silent and unknown, feel no need to express what they have experienced. Others devote their entire lives to the celebration of that "system beyond nature."

Is there anyone who can doubt that Igor Stravinsky is such a man?

BOOKS ABOUT
IGOR STRAVINSKY

BELAYEV, VICTOR. *Les Noces, An Outline*. London: Oxford University Press, 1928

CORLE, EDWIN (editor). *Igor Stravinsky*. New York: Duell, Sloan & Pearce (a Merle Armitage Book), 1946

LANG, PAUL HENRY. *Stravinsky: A New Appraisal of His Work*. New York: W. W. Norton, 1963

LEDERMAN, MINNA. *Stravinsky in the Theatre*. New York: Pellegrini & Cudahy, 1949

NEWMAN, ARNOLD (photos); CRAFT, ROBERT (text). *Bravo, Stravinsky!* New York: World Publishing Company, 1967

TANSMAN, ALEXANDRE. *Igor Stravinsky, The Man and His Music*. New York: G. P. Putnam's Sons, 1949

VLAD, ROMAN. *Stravinsky*. London and New York: Oxford University Press, 1960

WHITE, ERIC WALTER. *Stravinsky: The Composer and His Works*. Berkeley: University of California Press, 1966

BOOKS ABOUT
STRAVINSKY'S TIME

COLLAER, PAUL. *History of Modern Music*. New York: Grosset & Dunlap, Inc. (Universal Library), 1963

CONYN, CORNELIUS. *Three Centuries of Ballet*. Houston and New York: American Elsevier Publishing Company, Inc., 1953

FOKINE, MICHEL. *Memoirs of a Ballet Master*. Boston: Little, Brown and Company, 1961

LEONARD, RICHARD ANTHONY. *A History of Russian Music*. London: Jarrolds Publishers, Ltd., 1956

LIFAR, SERGE. *Serge Diaghilev: His Life, His Work, His Legend*. New York: G. P. Putnam's Sons, 1940

NIJINSKY, ROMOLA. *Nijinsky*. New York: Simon and Schuster, 1934

NIJINSKY, ROMOLA. *The Last Years of Nijinsky*. New York: Simon and Schuster, 1952

PRINCE LIEVEN, PETER. *The Birth of the Ballets Russes*. London: George Allen & Unwin, Ltd., 1956

THOMSON, VIRGIL. *Virgil Thomson*. New York: Alfred A. Knopf, 1966

YATES, PETER. *Twentieth-Century Music*. New York: Pantheon Books, 1967

BOOKS BY
IGOR STRAVINSKY

Chronicle of My Life. London: Victor Gollancz, Ltd.,
1936

An Autobiography. New York: Simon and Schuster,
1936, reprinted 1958. Paperback, W. W. Norton &
Company, 1962

Poetics of Music: In the Form of Six Lessons. Trans.
Arthur Knodel and Ingolf Dahl. Preface by Darius
Milhaud. Cambridge: Harvard University Press,
1947. New York: Random House, Vintage Books
paperback, 1956

Conversations with Igor Stravinsky. I. S. and Robert
Craft. New York: Doubleday & Company, Inc., 1959

Memories and Commentaries. I. S. and Robert Craft.
New York: Doubleday & Company, Inc., 1960

Expositions and Developments. I. S. and Robert Craft.
New York: Doubleday & Company, Inc., 1962

Dialogues and a Diary. I. S. and Robert Craft. New
York: Doubleday & Company, Inc., 1963

Themes and Episodes. I. S. and Robert Craft. New
York: Alfred A. Knopf, 1966

WORKS BY
IGOR STRAVINSKY

OPERAS

The Flood (Le Déluge). A Musical Play by Robert Craft. 1962

Mavra. Opera buffa in one act, after Pushkin, by Boris Kochno. 1922

The Nightingale (Le Rossignol). Lyric tale in three acts, after Hans Christian Andersen, by Igor Stravinsky and S. Mitusov. 1914

Oedipus Rex. Opera-oratorio in two acts, after Sophocles, by Igor Stravinsky and Jean Cocteau. 1927

The Rake's Progress. Opera by W. H. Auden and Chester Kallman. 1949–51.

BALLETS

Agon. 1957

Apollon Musagète (Apollo). 1928

The Fairy's Kiss (Le Baiser de la Fée). 1928

The Firebird. 1910

Les Noces. 1923

Orpheus. 1948
Perséphone. 1934
Pétrouchka. 1911
Pulcinella. 1920
The Rite of Spring (Le Sacre du Printemps). 1913

SYMPHONIC WORKS

Canon. On a Russian popular tune. 1965
Le Chant du Rossignol (The Song of the Nightingale). 1917
The Ebony Concerto. 1945
Fireworks. 1908
Four Studies for Orchestra. 1929
Greeting Prelude. For the eightieth birthday of Pierre Monteux. 1956
Monumentum. Three madrigals (c. 1600) by Gesualdo di Venosa, recomposed for instruments. 1960
Orpheus. 1948
Pétrouchka. 1910–11
Pulcinella. Suite. 1924
The Rite of Spring (Le Sacre du Printemps). 1911–13
Scherzo Fantastique. 1909
Symphonies of Wind Instruments. 1920
Variations for Orchestra. Aldous Huxley in memoriam. 1965
Violin Concerto. 1931

WORKS FOR STRING ORCHESTRA

Concerto in D ("Basle" Concerto). 1946

CONCERTOS FOR PIANO

Capriccio for Piano and Orchestra. 1929
Movements. 1958–59

WORKS FOR CHORUS AND ORCHESTRA

*J. S. Bach: Choral-Variationen über das Weihnachtslied
"Von Himmel Hoch da Komm Ich Her"* (From High
Heaven Come I). 1956
Cantata. 1952
Canticum Sacrum, Ad honorem Sancti Marci nominis
(In honor of the name of St. Mark). 1956
Introitus. T. S. Eliot in memoriam. 1965
Mass. 1948
Requiem Canticles. 1965–66
A Sermon, a Narrative, and a Prayer. 1960–61
Symphony of Psalms. 1930
Threni. 1957–58

WORKS FOR VOICE AND ORCHESTRA

Abraham and Isaac. 1962–63
In Memoriam Dylan Thomas. Dirge—canons and song.
1954
Mephistopheles' Lied vom Floh (The Song of the Flea).
Beethoven's arrangement (Op. 75, No. 3) of the
Goethe song, adapted by Stravinsky

Three Songs from William Shakespeare. 1953
Trois Petites Chansons. 1913
Trois Poésies de la Lyrique Japonaise. 1913
Two Poems by K. Balmont. 1911
Two Poems of Verlaine. 1910

INSTRUMENTAL MUSIC

Chanson Russe. 1922
Circus Polka. 1942
Double Canon. Raoul Dufy in memoriam. 1959
Duo Concertant. 1932
Elegy for J.F.K. 1964
Epitaphium. 1959
Fanfare for a New Theater. 1962
Histoire du Soldat. 1918
Octet for Wind Instruments. 1952
Ode. 1943
Septet. 1953
Serenade in A. 1925
Sonata. 1903–04
Three Pieces for String Quartet. 1914

SONGS

Anthem, "The Dove Descending Breaks the Air." 1962
Ave Maria. In Latin. 1949
Ave Maria. Church Slavonic version. 1934
Credo. In Latin. 1932
Illumina Nos. After Carlo Gesualdo di Venosa (c. 1600)

The Owl and the Pussycat. 1966
Pater Noster. In Latin. 1949
Pater Noster. Church Slavonic version. 1926
Russian Credo. 1964
Three Sacred Songs. 1957–59
Two Sacred Songs. Hugo Wolf/Stravinsky. 1969

FULL SCORES

Abraham and Isaac
Agon
Apollon Musagète (Apollo)
J. S. Bach: Choral-Variationen
Cantata
Canticum Sacrum
Capriccio for Piano and Orchestra
Chanson de Paracha (Russian Maiden's Song). From
   Mavra
Le Chant du Rossignol (The Song of the Nightingale)
Concerto in D ("Basle" Concerto)
Divertimento. Suite from *The Fairy's Kiss*
Double Canon
Epitaphium
The Fairy's Kiss
The Flood (Le Déluge)
Greeting Prelude
In Memoriam Dylan Thomas
Introitus
Mass
Monumentum

Movements
Octet for Wind Instruments
Oedipus Rex
Orpheus
Perséphone
Pétrouchka
Pulcinella. Complete
Pulcinella. Suite
Quatre Etudes pour Orchestre (Four Studies for Orchestra)
The Rake's Progress
Requiem Canticles
The Rite of Spring
Le Rossignol (The Nightingale)
Septet
A Sermon, a Narrative, and a Prayer
Symphonies of Wind Instruments
Symphony of Psalms
Three Songs from William Shakespeare
Threni
Trois Petites Chansons
Two Poems by K. Balmont and *Trois Poésies de la Lyrique Japonaise*
Two Poems of Verlaine
Variations for Orchestra

POCKET SCORES

Abraham and Isaac
Agon
Apollon Musagète (Apollo)
J. S. Bach: Choral-Variationen
Cantata
Canticum Sacrum
Capriccio for Piano and Orchestra
Le Chant du Rossignol (The Song of the Nightingale)
Concerto in D ("Basle" Concerto)
Divertimento
The Fairy's Kiss
Le Faune et la Bergère
The Flood (Le Déluge)
In Memoriam Dylan Thomas
Introitus
Mass
Monumentum
Movements
Octet for Wind Instruments
Oedipus Rex
Orpheus

Perséphone
Pétrouchka
Pulcinella. Suite
Quatre Etudes pour Orchestre (Four Studies for Orchestra)
The Rake's Progress
Requiem Canticles
The Rite of Spring
Le Rossignol (The Nightingale)
Septet
A Sermon, a Narrative, and a Prayer
Symphonies of Wind Instruments
Symphony of Psalms
Three Pieces for String Quartet
Three Songs from William Shakespeare
Threni
Variations for Orchestra

INDEX

ABOUT THE AUTHOR

Arnold Dobrin was born in Omaha, Nebraska, and has studied at the Chouinard Art Institute in Los Angeles, the University of California at Los Angeles, and the Académie de la Grande Chaumière in Paris. He lived in Rome for two years, and has traveled extensively in Europe, Asia, and the Near East.

Mr. Dobrin has written and illustrated many books for young readers on a wide variety of subjects, including a biography of another brilliant modern composer, Aaron Copland. With his wife and two young sons Mr. Dobrin now lives in Westport, Connecticut.